How To Quit Smoking:

The Ultimate Guide to Quitting Smoking and Reclaiming Your Health

Sarah Moore

Table of content

Introduction

In a small town of Clearwater, nestled amidst rolling green hills and crystal-clear lakes, there lived a young woman named Emily. She had grown up in a household where smoking was a common habit. Her parents, siblings, and even some of her closest friends were smokers. But as Emily entered her twenties, she realized that she wanted to break free from the grip of tobacco and embark on a smoke-free journey.

The decision was not an easy one for Emily, for she knew that breaking the chains of addiction would require determination, resilience, and support. She understood that it would be a challenging path, filled with temptations and moments of weakness. Nevertheless, she was ready to face the battle head-on and reclaim her health and happiness.

Emily sought out resources, gathering information on the dangers of smoking, the benefits of quitting, and the various methods available to help her along the way. Armed with knowledge, she decided to create a support system around herself, sharing her decision with her loved ones and seeking their understanding and encouragement.

Her family and friends were initially surprised by Emily's resolution, but they soon rallied around her with unwavering support. They understood the significance of her journey and were determined to stand by her side, offering encouragement and accountability whenever she needed it.

The day arrived when Emily took her first steps toward a smoke-free life. She gathered all her cigarettes, lighters, and ashtrays and disposed of them, bidding farewell to the familiar companions that had held her captive for so long. In their place, she filled her surroundings with reminders of her newfound commitment: fresh flowers, motivational quotes, and pictures of loved ones who inspired her.

The first few days were undoubtedly the most challenging. Emily experienced intense cravings and moments of doubt. But she turned to her support system, reaching out to her friends and family for encouragement. They listened to her frustrations, offered words of wisdom, and reminded her of the progress she had already made.

To keep her mind occupied and her hands busy, Emily delved into new hobbies and activities. She rediscovered her love for painting and spent hours creating vibrant canvases that depicted her journey towards freedom. She also began practicing yoga, finding solace in the deep breaths and peaceful stillness that replaced the once frequent puffs of smoke.

As time passed, Emily noticed subtle changes in her health and well-being. Her senses became sharper, and she could finally appreciate the aroma of freshly brewed coffee or the scent of blooming flowers. Her lungs began to breathe more freely, and her energy levels soared. These small victories served as constant reminders of the incredible transformation taking place within her.

Weeks turned into months, and Emily continued to build on her progress. She became an advocate for others seeking to break free from the chains of addiction, sharing her story and offering guidance to those who sought her help. Her journey had not only transformed her own life but also touched the lives of countless others.

As she reflected on her smoke-free journey, Emily marveled at the resilience of the human spirit. She had conquered her addiction, reclaimed her health, and inspired a community to follow in her footsteps. She knew that her journey was far from over, as she would continue to face challenges along the way. But armed with determination, unwavering support, and the knowledge that she was capable of creating a better future, Emily embraced each day with a renewed sense of purpose.

And so, with the sun setting over the tranquil town of Clearwater, Emily's smoke-free journey began, illuminating a path of hope and transformation for all who crossed her path.

Chapter 1

The Smoke-Free Journey Begins

Emily stood at the crossroads of her life, looking out at the vast horizon ahead. It was a pivotal moment, a turning point where she knew she had to make a decision that would shape her future. For years, she had been a prisoner to a habit that held her captive—the habit of smoking.

Born and raised in the town of Clearwater, Emily grew up surrounded by the lingering haze of smoke. It seemed as though everyone she knew indulged in this seemingly harmless yet insidious vice. But as she grew older, a desire burned within her—a desire to break free from the chains of addiction and embrace a healthier, smoke-free life.

The decision was not an easy one. Emily knew that giving up smoking would require immense willpower and dedication. She had tried before, only to succumb to the allure of nicotine's grip. But this time was different. This time, she had a plan—a roadmap to navigate the challenges that lay ahead.

Armed with determination, Emily began her journey by educating herself. She delved into books, articles, and personal stories of those who had triumphed over addiction. She learned about the detrimental effects of smoking on her health, the risks it posed to her loved ones through second-hand smoke, and the countless benefits of a smoke-free life.

Next, she surrounded herself with a support system. Emily shared her decision with her closest friends and family, opening up about her struggles and aspirations. To her surprise, they embraced her with unwavering encouragement and pledged to stand by her side, offering strength whenever she faltered.

With her newfound knowledge and support, Emily prepared herself mentally and emotionally for the challenges ahead. She knew that cravings would test her resolve, and there would be moments when she would be tempted to revert to old habits. But she was determined to stay the course, to forge a path of resilience and perseverance.

On the day she decided to quit, Emily bid farewell to her cigarettes and all remnants of her smoking habit. She cleared her surroundings of ashtrays, replacing them with reminders of her newfound commitment—a bowl of fresh fruit, a yoga mat for meditation, and a journal to document her progress.

The initial days were tough. Emily experienced withdrawal symptoms, battling intense cravings and moments of doubt. But she refused to let them consume her. She turned to her support system, reaching out to her loved ones when she needed encouragement or a listening ear. They reminded her of her strength, of the person she aspired to become.

To occupy her mind and distract herself from the allure of cigarettes, Emily threw herself into new hobbies. She joined a fitness class, discovering the joy of physical activity and the rush of endorphins that replaced the nicotine high. She immersed herself in creative pursuits, channeling her energy into painting and writing, finding solace in the therapeutic power of self-expression.

Days turned into weeks, weeks into months. Emily's journey continued, one step at a time. Gradually, she noticed the changes taking place within her. Her breathing became easier, her energy levels soared, and a newfound vibrancy filled her days. She marveled at the way her body and mind were healing, the resilience they possessed when given the chance.

But Emily's journey went beyond personal transformation. As she shared her story with others, she became an inspiration to those who also yearned to break free from the shackles of addiction. She joined support groups, volunteered at local clinics, and spoke at community events, spreading awareness about the dangers of smoking and the possibilities of a smoke-free life.

As Emily looked back on the path she had traveled, she realized that her smoke-free journey had become more than just a personal triumph—it had become a beacon of hope for others. She knew that challenges still lay ahead, but armed with the lessons she had learned and the unwavering support she had found, she was ready to face them head-on.

And so, standing at the crossroads of her life, Emily took her first steps towards a future free from smoke. The horizon shimmered with possibilities, and she walked forward with determination in her heart and a newfound lightness in her spirit. The journey had begun, and with every breath, she embraced the freedom she had longed for.

Smoking is widely recognized as a dangerous habit that poses numerous risks to both the smoker and those around them. Understanding these dangers is crucial for acknowledging the need for change and taking steps towards a healthier lifestyle. Here are some of the key dangers associated with smoking:

Health Risks: Smoking is the leading cause of preventable diseases and premature deaths worldwide. It significantly increases the risk of developing serious health conditions such as lung cancer, throat cancer, emphysema, chronic bronchitis, heart disease, stroke, and various respiratory illnesses. The chemicals in tobacco smoke harm nearly every organ in the body, leading to a range of health complications.

Secondhand Smoke: Not only does smoking harm the person directly inhaling the smoke, but it also poses a risk to those around them. Secondhand smoke contains over 7,000 chemicals, including at least 70 that can cause cancer. Exposure to secondhand smoke can lead to respiratory problems, cardiovascular disease, and an increased risk of lung cancer in non-smokers.

Addiction: Tobacco contains nicotine, a highly addictive substance. Nicotine addiction makes it difficult for smokers to quit even when they are aware of the associated health risks. The addiction can result in continued smoking despite adverse health effects and attempts to quit.

Financial Burden: Smoking is an expensive habit. The costs of purchasing cigarettes or other tobacco products can accumulate significantly over time. Additionally, smokers may face higher healthcare expenses due to smoking-related illnesses. Quitting smoking can lead to substantial savings and a more financially secure future.

Impact on Appearance: Smoking can negatively affect one's physical appearance. It can cause premature aging, wrinkles, stained teeth, bad breath, and a yellowish complexion. These cosmetic changes can impact self-esteem and confidence.

Acknowledging the need for change is the first step towards overcoming the dangers of smoking. Quitting smoking is not easy, but it is possible with determination and support. There are numerous resources available, such as nicotine replacement therapy, counseling, support groups, and medications, that can help individuals quit smoking and improve their overall health and well-being.

If you or someone you know is a smoker and wants to quit, it is important to seek professional help and support. Healthcare providers, smoking cessation programs, and organizations dedicated to tobacco control can provide guidance, tools, and encouragement throughout the quitting process. Remember, quitting smoking is a positive and life-changing decision that can greatly improve your health and quality of life.

Here are some additional points to consider:

Reduced Life Expectancy: Smoking significantly reduces life expectancy. On average, smokers live 10 years less than non-smokers. The toxins in tobacco smoke accelerate the aging process and damage vital organs, leading to a higher risk of premature death.

Impact on Mental Health: Smoking has been linked to various mental health issues, including increased rates of anxiety, depression, and stress. While some smokers may believe that smoking helps them cope with stress, it actually exacerbates these conditions in the long run.

Pregnancy Complications: Smoking during pregnancy poses serious risks to both the mother and the developing fetus. It increases the likelihood of complications such as premature birth, low birth weight, stillbirth, and sudden infant death syndrome (SIDS). It's crucial for expectant mothers to quit smoking to protect the health of themselves and their babies.

Environmental Impact: Cigarette smoking has adverse effects on the environment. Cigarette butts, which are the most commonly discarded form of litter, are not biodegradable and can contaminate water sources, harm wildlife, and contribute to pollution. Additionally, the production and transportation of tobacco products have environmental consequences, including deforestation and greenhouse gas emissions.

Social Impact: Smoking can have a negative impact on social interactions and relationships. The smell of smoke, secondhand smoke exposure, and the inconvenience of smoking restrictions can alienate non-smokers. Moreover, smoking is often not well-received in public spaces, which can lead to isolation and a sense of being marginalized.

It is essential to recognize the dangers of smoking and the need for change not only on an individual level but also at the societal level. Governments, public health organizations, and communities play a crucial role in implementing policies and programs that promote smoking cessation, tobacco control, and public awareness campaigns. By collectively addressing the dangers of smoking, we can create a healthier environment for everyone and reduce the prevalence of this harmful habit.

Setting a quit date and creating a personalized quit plan:

Setting a quit date and creating a personalized quit plan is an excellent step towards quitting a habit, such as smoking. Here are some steps to help you in the process:

Choose a Quit Date: Select a specific date within the next few weeks to quit smoking. Make sure it's a day when you can minimize stress and distractions as much as possible.

Identify Triggers: Recognize the situations, people, emotions, or activities that typically trigger your smoking habit. It could be stress, socializing, or certain places. Understanding your triggers will help you prepare strategies to deal with them effectively.

Seek Support: Inform your friends, family, and loved ones about your decision to quit smoking. Their support can make a significant difference during challenging times. You may also consider joining a support group or seeking professional help, such as counseling or therapy.

Create a Support Network: Surround yourself with people who have successfully quit smoking or those who are also trying to quit. Their experiences, advice, and encouragement can be invaluable in your journey.

Remove Temptation: Get rid of cigarettes, lighters, ashtrays, and anything else associated with smoking from your environment. Clean your home, car, and workplace to eliminate the smell of smoke. This can help reduce the urge to smoke.

Develop Coping Strategies: Find alternative ways to cope with cravings and withdrawal symptoms. You can try deep breathing exercises, engaging in physical activity, drinking water, chewing gum, or using nicotine replacement therapy if recommended by a healthcare professional.

Set Rewards and Milestones: Establish small goals and rewards for yourself along the way. Celebrate achievements such as one day, one week, or one month without smoking. Treat yourself to something you enjoy, like a movie or a spa day.

Prepare for Withdrawal Symptoms: Understand that withdrawal symptoms like irritability, anxiety, restlessness, and cravings are common when quitting smoking. Be prepared for them and remind yourself that they are temporary. They will gradually decrease over time.

Develop a Healthy Lifestyle: Focus on adopting a healthier lifestyle overall. Incorporate regular exercise, eat a balanced diet, and get enough sleep. Engaging in activities that promote well-being can help distract from cravings and improve your overall mood.

Stay Positive and Persistent: Quitting smoking can be challenging, but maintaining a positive attitude and staying persistent will increase your chances of success. Remind yourself of the reasons why you want to quit and the benefits you'll experience as a non-smoker.

Here are some additional steps you can take to enhance your quit plan:

Identify Personal Motivation: Reflect on why you want to quit smoking. Make a list of the reasons that are meaningful to you, such as improving your health, saving money, setting a positive example for loved ones, or regaining control over your life. Keep this list handy as a reminder of your motivation.

Track Your Smoking Habits: Keep a journal or use a smartphone app to track your smoking habits leading up to your quit date. Note the times when you smoke, the triggers that accompany each cigarette, and how you feel before and after smoking. This self-awareness will help you better understand your patterns and develop strategies to address them.

Develop a Plan for Cravings: Cravings can be intense during the quitting process. Identify specific strategies that work for you to manage cravings when they arise. This could include engaging in a hobby or activity, practicing mindfulness or meditation, or calling a supportive friend.

Explore Nicotine Replacement Therapy (NRT): If you're interested in using nicotine replacement products like patches, gum, lozenges, inhalers, or nasal sprays, consult with a healthcare professional. They can provide guidance on which form of NRT may be suitable for you and how to use it effectively.

Consider Medication Options: Certain prescription medications, such as bupropion (Zyban) and varenicline (Chantix), can assist with smoking cessation. Consult with a healthcare professional to discuss if medication is a suitable option for you and to understand the potential benefits and side effects.

Modify Your Routine: Identify the routines and habits that are closely associated with smoking, such as smoking during breaks or after meals. Modify these routines by replacing smoking with healthier alternatives. For example, you could take a walk, chew a piece of gum, or engage in deep breathing exercises instead of reaching for a cigarette.

Address Emotional Support: Quitting smoking can evoke various emotions, including stress, anxiety, or even sadness. It's essential to have emotional support in place during this time. Lean on trusted friends, family members, or a therapist to talk about your feelings and seek encouragement.

Educate Yourself: Learn about the health risks of smoking and the benefits of quitting. Understanding the positive impact quitting smoking can have on your overall health, including reducing the risk of various diseases, can serve as a strong motivator.

Stay Active and Engaged: Keeping yourself busy and engaged in activities can help distract from cravings. Plan activities that you enjoy, such as hobbies, exercise, or spending time with loved ones. Joining a support group or participating in a smoking cessation program can also provide structure and support.

Celebrate Milestones: Acknowledge and celebrate your achievements along the way. Set milestones and reward yourself when you reach them. Celebrating your progress reinforces positive behavior and boosts motivation to continue on your smoke-free journey.

Remember, quitting smoking is a personal journey, and everyone's experience is unique. Be patient and kind to yourself throughout the process. If you encounter challenges or setbacks, don't give up. Learn from them and use them as stepping stones to move forward. With dedication and perseverance, you can succeed in quitting smoking and lead a healthier, smoke-free life.

Identifying your smoking triggers:

Identifying smoking triggers is an essential step in understanding the factors that lead to smoking and developing strategies to overcome them. Here are some steps to help you identify your smoking triggers:

Keep a smoking journal: Start by keeping a journal to record each time you smoke. Note down the time, location, your mood, the people you are with, and any specific activities you were engaged in before lighting up a cigarette.

Recognize emotional triggers: Many people smoke as a way to cope with emotions such as stress, anxiety, boredom, or sadness. Pay attention to situations or feelings that tend to trigger the urge to smoke.

Identify social triggers: Smoking can often be associated with social situations or specific people. Note down instances when you tend to smoke more in the company of certain individuals or during social gatherings.

Track habitual triggers: Certain activities or routines can become strongly linked with smoking. For example, you may habitually smoke after a meal, while driving, or during work breaks. Identify these habitual triggers that prompt you to smoke.

Be mindful of environmental triggers: Environmental cues can also play a role in triggering the desire to smoke. These cues may include being in places where smoking is allowed, seeing cigarette advertisements, or even smelling the smoke from others.

Analyze patterns: After collecting data in your smoking journal for a sufficient period, review your entries and look for patterns or commonalities among your triggers. Pay attention to the most frequent triggers and those that have the strongest influence on your smoking behavior.

Create a plan: Once you have identified your smoking triggers, you can create a plan to manage and overcome them. Develop alternative strategies for dealing with the triggers, such as finding healthier ways to cope with emotions, avoiding smoking-related social situations, replacing smoking with a different activity during habitual triggers, or actively avoiding environmental cues that make you want to smoke.

Here are some additional tips and strategies to help you identify and manage your smoking triggers:

Involve others: Talk to your friends, family, or support groups about your efforts to identify your smoking triggers. They may provide valuable insights or help you recognize triggers that you may have overlooked.

Use technology: Consider using smartphone apps or digital tools designed to help you track your smoking habits and identify triggers. These apps often provide features like tracking smoking patterns, offering motivation and support, and suggesting alternative activities to distract you from smoking.

Assess your cravings: When you experience a craving for a cigarette, try to analyze what triggered it. Was it a specific situation, an emotion, or a habitual cue? Understanding the underlying cause of your cravings can help you address them more effectively.

Plan alternative activities: Identify healthy and enjoyable activities that can serve as alternatives to smoking when you encounter triggers. Engage in activities such as exercise, deep breathing exercises, reading, listening to music, or engaging in hobbies to distract yourself from the urge to smoke.

Make lifestyle changes: Consider making changes to your daily routines or environments to minimize exposure to triggers. For example, you could avoid places where smoking is prevalent, rearrange your living or working spaces to remove reminders of smoking, or find new social activities that do not revolve around smoking.

Seek professional help: If you're finding it challenging to identify or manage your smoking triggers on your own, consider seeking support from healthcare professionals or smoking cessation programs. They can provide personalized guidance, counseling, and additional resources to assist you in your quit smoking journey.

Stay motivated and persistent: Quitting smoking is a process that may involve setbacks along the way. Stay motivated, remind yourself of the reasons why you want to quit, and learn from any slip-ups. Each attempt brings you closer to successfully overcoming your smoking triggers.

Remember, quitting smoking is a highly individual process, and what works for one person may not work for another. It's important to find the strategies and techniques that resonate with you and support your journey towards a smoke-free life.

Chapter 2

The Science of Addiction

In Chapter 2 of our journey into the science of addiction, we delve into the transformative success story of Mark, a man who triumphed over the clutches of addiction to create a life filled with purpose and fulfillment. Mark's story serves as a testament to the power of resilience, support, and scientific understanding in overcoming addiction.

The Abyss of Addiction:
Mark's battle with addiction began in his late teens when he experimented with drugs as a way to cope with personal struggles and peer pressure. What initially seemed like occasional recreational use soon spiraled into a full-blown addiction, trapping him in a vicious cycle of substance abuse, withdrawal, and the desperate need for another fix. His life became a never-ending quest to satisfy an insatiable craving.

Hitting Rock Bottom:
As Mark's addiction tightened its grip, he began to experience severe consequences in various areas of his life. His physical health deteriorated, relationships crumbled, and he lost his job, which

only fueled his addiction further. He found himself isolated, trapped in a dark abyss with no apparent way out.

Seeking Help:
Despite the despair that consumed him, a glimmer of hope remained within Mark. Realizing that he couldn't overcome addiction alone, he mustered the courage to seek help. He reached out to a local addiction treatment center where professionals armed with the latest scientific knowledge were ready to guide him on his path to recovery.

Understanding the Science:
One crucial aspect of Mark's recovery was understanding the science behind addiction. Through educational sessions and individual counseling, he learned about the brain's reward system, the impact of substances on neurotransmitters, and the role of genetics and environment in addiction vulnerability. This knowledge not only empowered Mark but also helped him see addiction as a complex condition rather than a personal failing.

Building a Support Network:
Another critical element in Mark's success story was the establishment of a strong support network. Alongside professional help, he found solace in connecting with others who had gone through similar struggles. Group therapy sessions and support groups allowed Mark to share his experiences, learn from

others, and gain the emotional support necessary for his recovery journey.

Embracing a Holistic Approach:
Mark's recovery journey was not limited to addressing his substance abuse alone. He discovered the importance of adopting a holistic approach to healing, which involved addressing his physical, mental, and emotional well-being. Through therapy, exercise, nutrition, and self-care practices, he began to rebuild his life from the ground up, nurturing a sense of wholeness he hadn't experienced in years.

The Power of Resilience:
Throughout his recovery, Mark encountered setbacks and faced numerous challenges. Relapses occurred, and moments of doubt crept in. However, armed with a newfound resilience and armed with the scientific knowledge of addiction, he persevered. Each setback became a learning opportunity, enabling him to strengthen his resolve and deepen his commitment to a life free from addiction.

Embracing a Life of Fulfillment:
As Mark's recovery journey progressed, he discovered new passions and interests. He pursued further education, focusing on a career that allowed him to support others facing similar challenges. Mark became a beacon of hope for those still trapped in the clutches of addiction, sharing his story, and advocating for

greater understanding and support for individuals on the path to recovery.

Conclusion:
Mark's success story illuminates the transformative power of scientific understanding, resilience, and support in overcoming addiction. By embracing the science of addiction and building a robust support network, Mark not only conquered his own battles but also became an inspiration to others. His journey reminds us that no matter how deep the abyss of addiction may seem, there is always hope for a brighter future.

Demystifying nicotine addiction:
Nicotine addiction is a complex process that involves both physical and psychological factors. Here's a breakdown of the key aspects involved in understanding and demystifying nicotine addiction:

Nicotine and the brain: Nicotine is a naturally occurring chemical found in tobacco products. When nicotine enters the body, it binds to nicotine receptors in the brain, specifically in the areas responsible for reward and pleasure. This interaction triggers the release of neurotransmitters like dopamine, which creates a pleasurable sensation.

Physical dependence: Nicotine is highly addictive, and continued use leads to physical dependence. Over time, the brain adapts to the presence of nicotine by reducing the number of nicotine receptors, leading to tolerance. As a result, individuals require higher doses of nicotine to achieve the same effects, leading to a cycle of increased use.

Withdrawal symptoms: When a person addicted to nicotine attempts to quit or reduce their intake, they may experience withdrawal symptoms. These symptoms can include cravings, irritability, anxiety, difficulty concentrating, increased appetite, and sleep disturbances. Withdrawal symptoms vary in intensity and duration, depending on individual factors such as the level of addiction and quitting methods.

Psychological factors: Nicotine addiction also has a significant psychological component. Smoking or using nicotine products can become associated with various activities or emotions, such as stress relief, socializing, or relaxation. These associations create strong psychological cravings, making it challenging to quit.

Social and environmental influences: Nicotine addiction can be influenced by social and environmental factors. Peer pressure, family history of smoking, cultural norms, advertising, and availability of tobacco products all play a role in initiating and perpetuating addiction.

Nicotine replacement therapy (NRT): NRT products, such as patches, gum, lozenges, inhalers, or nasal sprays, provide controlled doses of nicotine without the harmful chemicals found in tobacco smoke. NRT can help manage withdrawal symptoms and gradually reduce nicotine dependence.

Behavioral and psychosocial interventions: Quitting smoking or overcoming nicotine addiction often requires a combination of pharmacological treatments and behavioral interventions. These may include counseling, support groups, cognitive-behavioral therapy (CBT), and other strategies to address the psychological aspects of addiction.

Long-term effects: Nicotine addiction can have severe health consequences. It is linked to various diseases, including cardiovascular disorders, respiratory problems, and certain types of cancer. Quitting smoking or using nicotine products significantly reduces the risks and improves overall health outcomes.

Demystifying nicotine addiction involves understanding the physiological and psychological factors involved, recognizing the impact of social and environmental influences, and implementing comprehensive strategies to address both physical dependence and psychological cravings. Seeking professional help, such as from healthcare providers or smoking cessation programs, can greatly assist individuals in overcoming nicotine addiction.

Here are some additional points to further demystify nicotine addiction:

Nicotine and tolerance: Continued nicotine use leads to an increased tolerance, requiring higher doses to achieve the same effect. This process contributes to the cycle of addiction and makes quitting more challenging.

Nicotine and the reward system: Nicotine stimulates the release of dopamine, a neurotransmitter associated with pleasure and reward. This reinforcement of pleasurable feelings strengthens the brain's association between nicotine use and positive experiences, contributing to addiction.

Nicotine and stress: Many individuals turn to nicotine as a means of coping with stress. Nicotine can temporarily reduce anxiety and tension, leading to a perceived stress-relief effect. However, this relief is short-lived and can create a cycle where nicotine use becomes intertwined with managing stress.

Dual addiction: Nicotine addiction often co-occurs with other substance use disorders. Individuals addicted to nicotine may also have an increased susceptibility to developing addiction to other substances, such as alcohol or illicit drugs.

Nicotine and mental health: There is a strong correlation between nicotine addiction and mental health conditions. People with mental illnesses, such as depression, anxiety disorders, or attention-deficit/hyperactivity disorder (ADHD), are more likely to smoke and face greater challenges in quitting.

Nicotine and cues/triggers: Nicotine addiction involves conditioned responses to various cues or triggers. These can be environmental, social, or emotional factors that become associated with nicotine use. For example, a person may experience cravings when they encounter specific situations, such as drinking coffee or being around friends who smoke.

Relapse and quitting: Nicotine addiction is challenging to overcome, and relapse is common during the quitting process. It's important to understand that relapse doesn't mean failure but rather serves as an opportunity to learn from the experience and refine quitting strategies.

Harm reduction approaches: For individuals who are unable or unwilling to quit nicotine completely, harm reduction approaches can be helpful. These approaches focus on minimizing the health risks associated with nicotine use by transitioning to less harmful nicotine delivery methods, such as electronic cigarettes (vaping) or snus.

Support and resources: Quitting nicotine addiction is more successful when individuals have access to support and resources. Various organizations, hotlines, support groups, and online communities are available to provide guidance, encouragement, and practical strategies for quitting.

Personalized approaches: Every individual's journey with nicotine addiction is unique. Tailoring quitting strategies to individual preferences, circumstances, and level of addiction increases the likelihood of success. Combining multiple approaches, such as medication, therapy, and support systems, can optimize outcomes.

Remember, overcoming nicotine addiction is challenging but entirely possible with the right support, determination, and personalized approach. Seeking professional help and building a support network can significantly increase the chances of successfully quitting and improving overall health and well-being.

Exploring the physiological and psychological effects of smoking:

Smoking has well-documented physiological and psychological effects on individuals. Let's explore both aspects in more detail:

Physiological Effects of Smoking:
Cardiovascular System: Smoking is a major risk factor for cardiovascular diseases. It damages blood vessels, increases blood pressure, reduces oxygen supply to tissues, and promotes the

formation of blood clots. These effects can lead to conditions such as heart disease, stroke, and peripheral vascular disease.

Respiratory System: Smoking is a primary cause of various respiratory problems. It damages the airways and lung tissue, leading to chronic bronchitis, emphysema, and an increased risk of developing respiratory infections like pneumonia. Smoking is the leading cause of lung cancer.

Immune System: Smoking weakens the immune system, making individuals more susceptible to infections, including respiratory infections and delayed wound healing.

Reproductive System: Smoking can have detrimental effects on reproductive health. It increases the risk of infertility, erectile dysfunction in males, and complications during pregnancy, such as ectopic pregnancy, premature birth, and low birth weight.

Cancer: Smoking is strongly associated with an increased risk of various cancers, including lung, throat, mouth, esophageal, bladder, kidney, and pancreatic cancer.

Psychological Effects of Smoking:

Addiction: Nicotine, a highly addictive substance present in tobacco, is primarily responsible for the addictive nature of smoking. It activates the brain's reward system, leading to dependence and cravings. Quitting smoking can result in withdrawal symptoms, including irritability, anxiety, and difficulty concentrating.

Mood and Mental Health: Many smokers report experiencing psychological benefits from smoking, such as stress relief, relaxation, and improved mood. However, these effects are temporary and often result from the relief of nicotine withdrawal symptoms. In the long term, smoking is associated with increased risk for mental health conditions such as anxiety disorders and depression.

Social and Behavioral Factors: Smoking often becomes a social activity, leading to social bonding among smokers. It can also become a coping mechanism for stress or an emotional crutch. Additionally, smoking habits can be influenced by environmental cues and situations, making it challenging to quit.

It's important to note that the negative physiological and psychological effects of smoking are well-documented, and quitting smoking is highly beneficial for overall health and well-being. Seeking support from healthcare professionals, utilizing cessation programs, and adopting healthier alternatives can significantly improve health outcomes for individuals who smoke.

Here are some additional details about the physiological and psychological effects of smoking:

Physiological Effects of Smoking:

Respiratory Symptoms: Smoking can cause chronic coughing, wheezing, and shortness of breath. These symptoms can be particularly pronounced in individuals with conditions such as asthma or chronic obstructive pulmonary disease (COPD).

Reduced Lung Function: Smoking damages the lungs and impairs lung function. It reduces the lungs' ability to expand and contract efficiently, leading to decreased lung capacity and decreased overall respiratory function.

Increased Risk of Chronic Diseases: Smoking is linked to various chronic diseases beyond cardiovascular disease and cancer. These include chronic obstructive pulmonary disease (COPD), which encompasses conditions such as chronic bronchitis and emphysema, as well as conditions like diabetes, rheumatoid arthritis, and age-related macular degeneration.

Psychological Effects of Smoking:

Psychological Dependency: In addition to the physical addiction to nicotine, smoking can create a strong psychological dependency. People often associate smoking with certain activities or situations, which can make it challenging to quit. For example, individuals may feel the urge to smoke when socializing, during breaks, or when dealing with stress.

Self-Perception and Identity: Smoking can become ingrained in a person's self-perception and identity, especially if they have been smoking for a long time. Quitting smoking may involve challenging these perceptions and finding new ways to define oneself.

Body Image and Social Perception: Smoking has been portrayed as glamorous or socially desirable in the past, though societal attitudes have shifted significantly. Nonetheless, some individuals may still associate smoking with a certain image or social status. Quitting smoking may involve addressing concerns about body image or the fear of losing social connections.

Psychological Distress: Although some smokers may report feeling a sense of relaxation or stress relief while smoking, research suggests that smoking is associated with higher levels of psychological distress, anxiety, and depression. This may be due to the addictive nature of smoking, the health consequences, and the impact on overall well-being.

It's crucial to recognize that while smoking can provide temporary relief or perceived benefits in certain situations, the long-term health risks and negative consequences outweigh any potential advantages. Quitting smoking has numerous health benefits, including improved lung function, reduced risk of diseases, increased life expectancy, and improved overall well-being. There are various resources available, such as counseling, support groups, nicotine replacement therapy, and medications, to help individuals quit smoking successfully.

Understanding the brain's reward system and how it relates to smoking:
The brain's reward system plays a significant role in addiction, including smoking. To understand this connection, let's delve into the basics of the brain's reward system and its relationship with smoking.

The brain's reward system is a complex network of brain regions that are involved in reinforcing behaviors that are pleasurable or rewarding. It is primarily regulated by a neurotransmitter called dopamine, which is released in response to rewarding stimuli. Dopamine helps to create feelings of pleasure, motivation, and reinforcement, thereby encouraging behaviors that lead to the activation of the reward system.

When a person smokes, nicotine, a highly addictive substance found in tobacco, rapidly enters the bloodstream and reaches the brain. In the brain, nicotine interacts with receptors that are normally activated by a neurotransmitter called acetylcholine. This interaction leads to the release of dopamine in the brain's reward system.

Dopamine release in response to nicotine reinforces the behavior of smoking. It creates a pleasurable sensation and a sense of reward, which encourages individuals to continue smoking. Over time, the brain adapts to the presence of nicotine, and the reward system becomes increasingly dependent on it. This process contributes to the development of addiction, making it difficult for individuals to quit smoking.

Repeated exposure to nicotine and the subsequent release of dopamine lead to neuroadaptations in the brain. These adaptations alter the structure and function of the reward system and other brain regions involved in decision-making, impulse control, and self-regulation. As a result, individuals may experience cravings, tolerance (requiring higher doses of nicotine to achieve the same effect), withdrawal symptoms when attempting to quit, and an increased likelihood of relapse.

It is important to note that the brain's reward system is not the sole factor in smoking addiction. There are other psychological, social, and environmental factors that contribute to the initiation and maintenance of smoking habits. However, the rewarding effects of nicotine on the brain's reward system are a crucial aspect of the addictive nature of smoking.

Understanding the brain's reward system and its relationship with smoking provides insights into the challenges faced by individuals trying to quit smoking. Effective smoking cessation strategies often involve addressing the physiological and psychological aspects of addiction, providing support, and employing techniques to manage cravings and withdrawal symptoms.

Here are some additional insights regarding the brain's reward system and its relationship with smoking:

Reinforcement and Conditioning: The brain's reward system is involved in reinforcement and conditioning processes. When a behavior, such as smoking, is 0consistently associated with the release of dopamine and pleasurable sensations, it creates a strong association between the behavior and the reward. This association strengthens over time, making it more difficult to break the habit.

Cravings and Triggers: The brain's reward system plays a role in generating cravings for nicotine. Exposure to cues associated with smoking, such as seeing a pack of cigarettes or being in a social setting where others are smoking, can trigger a release of dopamine and activate the craving for nicotine. These cravings can be intense and difficult to resist, contributing to the cycle of addiction.

Pleasure vs. Relief: While the initial experiences of smoking are often pleasurable, with repeated use, smoking can also provide relief from withdrawal symptoms caused by nicotine dependence. The brain's reward system reinforces this relief by associating smoking with the alleviation of discomfort, making it a self-perpetuating cycle.

Sensitization: Prolonged exposure to nicotine can lead to a process called sensitization, where the brain's reward system becomes hypersensitive to the effects of nicotine. This can intensify the reinforcing properties of smoking and make it even more difficult to quit.

Interplay with Other Substances: The brain's reward system is not exclusive to smoking but is involved in the processing of rewards from various sources. However, the interaction between nicotine and the reward system can have unique effects. For example, nicotine can enhance the release of dopamine more rapidly and reliably than other natural rewards, making it highly addictive.

Withdrawal and Anhedonia: When someone tries to quit smoking, they may experience withdrawal symptoms as the brain readjusts to the absence of nicotine. These symptoms can include irritability, anxiety, difficulty concentrating, and depressed mood. This period of withdrawal is often characterized by anhedonia, the inability to experience pleasure, as the brain's reward system is temporarily dysregulated.

Understanding the intricate relationship between the brain's reward system and smoking addiction helps researchers and healthcare professionals develop strategies to effectively address nicotine dependence. By targeting the reward pathways and providing support through counseling, medication, and behavioral interventions, individuals can increase their chances of successfully quitting smoking and managing cravings in the long term.

Chapter 3

Overcoming Mental Barriers

In a world filled with limitless possibilities, success often eludes those held captive by their own mental barriers. Such was the case for Emma, a young aspiring entrepreneur who found herself trapped in a cycle of self-doubt and fear. But through resilience, determination, and a burning desire for personal growth, she shattered the shackles of her own mind and embarked on a remarkable journey towards success.

Emma's story begins in a small town, where she grew up surrounded by dreams and ambitions that seemed out of reach. As a child, she possessed an innate curiosity and a thirst for knowledge, but she also carried the burden of self-imposed limitations. Doubts plagued her every step, whispering incessantly that she was not capable of achieving greatness.

Despite these barriers, Emma held onto a glimmer of hope. She knew deep within her heart that she was meant for something more, something beyond the boundaries of her own imagination. With this flicker of determination, she resolved to confront her fears head-on.

Emma started by challenging her negative self-talk. Instead of succumbing to doubt, she embraced affirmations and positive thinking. Every morning, she looked at herself in the mirror and repeated, "I am capable of achieving anything I set my mind to." Gradually, the power of these words began to take hold, reshaping her mindset and laying the foundation for her success.

The next step in Emma's journey was to confront her fear of failure. She understood that failure was not an endpoint but rather a stepping stone on the path to success. Embracing the motto "fail forward," she took risks and learned from each setback. Whether it was starting a business, pursuing a new skill, or launching a creative project, Emma dove headfirst into the unknown, unafraid of the possibility of stumbling.

To further fortify her mental resilience, Emma sought out mentors and like-minded individuals who shared her passion for personal growth. She surrounded herself with a supportive network of individuals who believed in her abilities and challenged her to reach higher. Their collective wisdom, encouragement, and unwavering belief in her potential propelled Emma forward, even during moments of self-doubt.

As Emma persisted on her journey, she discovered that success wasn't merely an external achievement but an internal transformation. She realized that her mental barriers were nothing more than illusions, self-imposed limitations that had held her back for far too long. With each obstacle she overcame, her confidence grew, and her capacity for greatness expanded.

Over time, Emma's perseverance paid off in unimaginable ways. She launched a successful startup that revolutionized the industry, using her unique perspective and unwavering belief in herself to disrupt the status quo. She became a sought-after public speaker, sharing her story and empowering others to overcome their mental barriers. Emma's journey was not without its challenges, but she faced them head-on, transforming adversity into fuel for her success.

In the end, Emma's success story serves as a testament to the power of the human spirit and the ability to overcome mental barriers. By conquering her doubts, embracing failure as a catalyst for growth, and surrounding herself with a supportive network, she shattered the constraints that had held her back. Her journey is a reminder to us all that success is not determined by external circumstances, but by our ability to overcome the barriers within our own minds.

And so, as we close this chapter on overcoming mental barriers, let Emma's story inspire and motivate us to break free from the confines of self-doubt, for within each of us lies the potential to achieve greatness beyond our wildest dreams.

Challenging common myths and misconceptions about quitting:

Myth 1: Quitting is a sign of weakness.
Reality: Quitting can actually be a sign of strength and self-awareness. Recognizing when something is not serving you well or aligning with your goals and having the courage to make a change takes self-reflection and the willingness to prioritize your well-being.

Myth 2: Quitting means you've failed.
Reality: Quitting does not always equate to failure. Sometimes, circumstances change, priorities shift, or new opportunities arise that require you to let go of something. Quitting can be a strategic decision to redirect your efforts towards more fulfilling or rewarding endeavors.

Myth 3: Quitting is always a bad thing.
Reality: Quitting can be a positive and empowering choice. If a certain activity or commitment no longer brings you joy, causes excessive stress, or hinders your personal growth, quitting can be a way to regain control of your life and focus on what truly matters to you.

Myth 4: Quitting means you haven't given it enough effort.
Reality: Effort is important, but it's equally important to assess whether your efforts are yielding the desired results or

contributing to your overall well-being. Sometimes, despite your best efforts, a situation may not improve or align with your values. In such cases, quitting can be a wise decision that allows you to explore alternative paths.

Myth 5: Quitting will lead to regret.
Reality: While it's natural to feel some sense of loss or disappointment after quitting, it doesn't necessarily mean you will regret your decision. By quitting, you create opportunities for growth, self-discovery, and finding new paths that may ultimately lead to greater fulfillment and happiness.

Myth 6: Quitting is easy.
Reality: Quitting can be challenging, especially if you have invested a significant amount of time, effort, or emotions into something. It may involve overcoming fear, societal pressure, or the fear of judgment from others. However, prioritizing your well-being and personal growth often outweigh the temporary challenges associated with quitting.

Myth 7: Quitting is a permanent decision.
Reality: Quitting doesn't always mean closing the door forever. In some cases, quitting may be a temporary break or a way to reassess and make necessary adjustments. You can always revisit a situation later with a fresh perspective and new insights gained from the experience remember, quitting should be a thoughtful and intentional decision. It's essential to consider the implication the

pros and cons, and seek advice or support from necessary. Ultimately, only you can determine what is best for your own well-being and personal growth.

Myth 8: Quitting means you're letting others down.
Reality: While it's natural to consider the impact of your decision on others, it's important to prioritize your own well-being and personal growth. Staying in a situation that is detrimental to your mental, emotional, or physical health can ultimately hinder your ability to be there for others in a meaningful way.

Myth 9: Quitting is always a last resort.
Reality: Quitting doesn't have to be a last resort. It can be a proactive choice to create positive change in your life. Recognizing when something is not aligning with your goals, values, or aspirations and making the decision to quit can lead to new opportunities and personal growth.

Myth 10: Quitting means you're abandoning your responsibilities.
Reality: While it's important to fulfill your commitments and responsibilities, it's equally important to recognize when a situation is no longer sustainable or healthy. Quitting can be a responsible choice when it allows you to prioritize your well-being and find alternative solutions that are more suitable for all parties involved.

Myth 11: Quitting is a quick fix for all problems.

Reality: Quitting should be a well-considered decision, but it's not a cure-all for every challenge or difficulty you may encounter. It's important to assess the situation, explore potential solutions, and consider the long-term consequences before deciding to quit.

Myth 12: Quitting is a sign of lack of perseverance.

Reality: Perseverance is important, but it's equally important to recognize when to persevere and when to make a change. Quitting can be an act of self-awareness and adaptability, demonstrating that you have the ability to assess situations realistically and make decisions that align with your well-being and goals.

Myth 13: Quitting means you've wasted your time.

Reality: The time invested in a particular endeavor is not necessarily wasted just because you decide to quit. Every experience, even if it doesn't result in the desired outcome, can provide valuable lessons, skills, or insights that can be applied to future endeavors.

Myth 14: Quitting is only acceptable in extreme circumstances.

Reality: Quitting can be a valid choice in various circumstances, not just extreme situations. Whether it's leaving a toxic relationship, ending a job that doesn't fulfill you, or quitting a hobby that no longer brings joy, recognizing when to let go is an important aspect of personal growth and well-being.

Remember, quitting is a personal decision that should be based on your unique circumstances, values, and goals. It's important to trust your intuition, seek guidance when needed, and have the courage to make choices that support your overall well-being and happiness.

Cultivating a smoke-free mindset:

Cultivating a smoke-free mindset involves adopting a positive and determined approach to quitting smoking and maintaining a smoke-free lifestyle. Here are some strategies to help you develop and reinforce a smoke-free mindset:

Set a Clear Goal: Define your reasons for wanting to quit smoking and set a specific goal. It could be improving your health, saving money, being a role model for loved ones, or regaining control over your life. Make sure your goal is personal and meaningful to you.

Educate Yourself: Learn about the harmful effects of smoking and the benefits of quitting. Understanding the risks and rewards can strengthen your resolve to stay smoke-free.

Create a Quit Plan: Develop a comprehensive plan to quit smoking. Consider using nicotine replacement therapy, seeking professional help, or joining a support group. Having a structured plan in place increases your chances of success.

Identify Triggers: Recognize the situations, people, or emotions that typically trigger your smoking habit. Common triggers include stress, socializing with smokers, or certain places. Once you identify them, strategize ways to cope with these triggers effectively.

Change Your Environment: Modify your surroundings to minimize the temptation to smoke. Get rid of cigarettes, lighters, and ashtrays in your home, car, and workplace. Surround yourself with supportive people who encourage your smoke-free lifestyle.

Practice Mindfulness and Relaxation Techniques: Develop healthy coping mechanisms to manage cravings and stress. Deep breathing exercises, meditation, yoga, or engaging in hobbies and activities you enjoy can help distract and calm your mind.

Stay Positive and Persistent: Be kind to yourself during the quitting process. Recognize that quitting smoking is challenging, and setbacks may occur. If you slip up, don't be discouraged. Treat it as a learning experience and renew your commitment to staying smoke-free.

Celebrate Milestones: Acknowledge and celebrate your achievements along the way. Set smaller milestones and reward yourself for reaching them. Celebrating your progress reinforces positive behavior and motivates you to continue.

Seek Support: Don't hesitate to reach out for support from friends, family, or professionals. Share your goals and progress with them, and let them be a source of encouragement during challenging times.

Visualize a Smoke-Free Future: Imagine your life as a non-smoker and focus on the benefits it will bring. Visualize yourself enjoying improved health, increased energy, and a sense of freedom from smoking. This mental image can reinforce your commitment to a smoke-free lifestyle.

Here are some additional strategies for cultivating a smoke-free mindset:

Keep a Journal: Maintain a journal to track your progress, record your thoughts and emotions, and document the positive changes you experience as a non-smoker. This can serve as a powerful reminder of your journey and motivate you to continue on the smoke-free path.

Find Healthy Alternatives: Replace smoking with healthier habits and activities. Engage in regular exercise to release endorphins, which can help reduce cravings and improve your mood. Explore new hobbies, such as painting, cooking, or playing a musical instrument, to occupy your time and distract from thoughts of smoking.

Engage in Supportive Communities: Connect with others who are also on a smoke-free journey. Join online forums, support groups, or social media communities where you can share experiences, seek advice, and receive encouragement from like-minded individuals. Surrounding yourself with a supportive community can significantly boost your motivation and determination.

Visualize the Consequences: Imagine the negative consequences of continuing to smoke. Picture the impact on your health, relationships, and overall well-being. By vividly visualizing these consequences, you reinforce your commitment to a smoke-free life.

Practice Self-Care: Prioritize self-care activities to reduce stress and nurture your well-being. Engage in activities that bring you joy and relaxation, such as taking warm baths, reading a book, listening to music, or spending quality time with loved ones. Taking care of yourself holistically can strengthen your resolve to remain smoke-free.

Seek Professional Help: If you're finding it challenging to quit smoking or maintain a smoke-free lifestyle, consider reaching out to healthcare professionals or smoking cessation programs. They can provide personalized guidance, support, and additional resources to assist you in your journey.

Learn from Relapses: If you do experience a relapse, don't be too hard on yourself. Instead, view it as an opportunity to learn from the experience. Reflect on what triggered the relapse and develop strategies to handle similar situations better in the future. Remember, quitting smoking is a process, and setbacks can be valuable learning moments on the path to long-term success.

Stay Informed: Stay updated on the latest research, studies, and information related to smoking and quitting methods. Knowledge can empower you and strengthen your resolve to stay smoke-free. Being aware of the benefits and advancements in smoking cessation can further reinforce your decision to quit.

Set New Goals: Once you have successfully quit smoking, set new goals to maintain your smoke-free lifestyle. This could include improving your fitness level, pursuing a new career, or participating in a charity event. Setting and achieving new goals can provide a sense of purpose and motivation, helping you stay committed to your smoke-free mindset.

Celebrate Your Success: Celebrate your milestones and successes regularly. Treat yourself to rewards that are unrelated to smoking, such as a massage, a day trip, or a special gift. Celebrating your accomplishments reinforces your positive behavior and reminds you of the progress you've made.

Remember, developing a smoke-free mindset is an ongoing process, and it requires commitment, patience, and perseverance. Be kind to yourself, stay focused on your goals, and leverage the support and resources available to you. With time and determination, you can cultivate a mindset that supports a healthy and smoke-free life.

Harnessing the power of positive affirmations and visualization techniques:

Positive affirmations and visualization techniques are powerful tools that can help individuals harness their thoughts and beliefs to create positive change in their lives. By consciously focusing on positive affirmations and using visualization techniques, you can align your mindset with your desired outcomes and increase your chances of achieving them. Here's a breakdown of each technique:

Positive Affirmations:

Positive affirmations involve consciously repeating positive statements to yourself. By regularly affirming positive beliefs, you can reprogram your subconscious mind and shift your mindset towards success and abundance. Here are some key points to keep in mind when using positive affirmations:

Be specific: Formulate affirmations that clearly state what you want to achieve or the qualities you want to embody. For example, instead of saying, "I am successful," you can say, "I am a successful entrepreneur who is thriving in my business."

Use present tense: Phrase your affirmations as if you have already achieved your desired outcome. This helps your subconscious mind accept and integrate them more effectively.

Believe and feel: It's crucial to believe in the affirmations you repeat and evoke the corresponding emotions. This strengthens the impact of the affirmations on your subconscious mind.

Consistency is key: Practice affirmations regularly, ideally on a daily basis. Repeat them aloud or silently, and reinforce them with conviction and positivity.

Visualization:

Visualization is a technique that involves creating vivid mental images of yourself achieving your goals or embodying your desired qualities. Visualization helps you tap into the power of your imagination and stimulates your subconscious mind to work towards manifesting your aspirations. Here are some guidelines for effective visualization:

Relaxation: Find a quiet and comfortable space where you can relax without distractions. Deep breathing exercises or meditation can help you achieve a calm state before visualizing.

Detailed imagery: Visualize your desired outcomes or qualities with as much detail as possible. Engage all your senses and make the image as vivid and real as you can.

Emotional connection: As you visualize, connect with the emotions you would experience when you achieve your goals. Feel the joy, satisfaction, or excitement associated with your success.

Practice regularly: Dedicate time each day to practice visualization. Consistency and repetition are essential for reprogramming your subconscious mind and reinforcing positive beliefs.

Combining positive affirmations and visualization techniques amplifies their effectiveness. By repeating positive affirmations while vividly visualizing your desired outcomes, you reinforce your beliefs and align your subconscious mind with your conscious goals. Remember, these techniques are most effective when combined with proactive action and a mindset of perseverance and growth.

Here are some additional tips and strategies to enhance the power of positive affirmations and visualization techniques:

Personalize Your Affirmations: Tailor your affirmations to align with your specific goals, desires, and values. Make them meaningful and relevant to your life and aspirations. This personalization increases the emotional resonance and connection with your affirmations.

Use Affirmations for Self-Improvement: In addition to using affirmations for achieving specific goals, incorporate affirmations that promote personal growth, self-confidence, self-love, and resilience. This broader focus can help you develop a positive mindset overall.

Practice Gratitude: Integrate gratitude into your affirmations and visualizations. Expressing gratitude for what you have and what you have already achieved helps shift your focus towards abundance and attract more positivity into your life.

Create Visual Boards or Vision Journals: Visual boards, also known as vision boards, or vision journals are physical or digital collages of images, words, and affirmations that represent your goals and desires. They serve as a visual reminder of your aspirations and can enhance the effectiveness of your visualization practice.

Engage Your Emotions: When visualizing, try to evoke strong positive emotions associated with achieving your goals. Emotional engagement adds depth and intensity to your visualizations, making them more impactful.

Incorporate Meditation: Combine affirmations and visualizations with meditation practices. Meditation helps calm the mind, increases focus, and enhances the connection between your conscious and subconscious mind. You can recite your affirmations during meditation or visualize your desired outcomes in a deep state of relaxation.

Create Affirmation Rituals: Establish specific times during your day when you repeat your affirmations. It could be upon waking up, before going to bed, or during dedicated meditation or reflection sessions. Consistency and repetition are key to reinforcing positive beliefs.

Believe in the Process: Cultivate a genuine belief in the power of positive affirmations and visualization techniques. Trust that they can influence your thoughts, beliefs, and actions, leading to positive changes in your life. A positive mindset and faith in the process increase the effectiveness of these techniques.

Remember that positive affirmations and visualization techniques work best when combined with consistent action towards your goals. Take inspired steps, make decisions aligned with your aspirations, and remain open to opportunities that come your way. By harnessing the power of positive affirmations and visualization, you can foster a mindset of success, attract positive outcomes, and manifest your desired reality.

Chapter 4

Effective Quitting Strategies

In this chapter, we will explore the inspiring success story of Lisa, a former smoker who successfully quit smoking after many years of struggling with the habit. Lisa's journey highlights the effectiveness of various quitting strategies and offers valuable insights for individuals seeking to overcome their own addictions. By examining the key elements of Lisa's success, we can gain a deeper understanding of the effective quitting strategies that can be applied to various habits or dependencies.

Lisa's Smoking Addiction:

Lisa began smoking in her early twenties, initially viewing it as a social activity. However, what started as an occasional indulgence gradually transformed into a full-blown addiction. As the years passed, Lisa found herself increasingly dependent on cigarettes to manage stress, socialize, and cope with her emotions. Despite numerous attempts to quit smoking, she always found herself relapsing, feeling defeated and trapped by her addiction.

The Turning Point:

The turning point for Lisa came when she experienced a health scare that forced her to confront the harsh reality of the consequences of her habit. She realized that her smoking was negatively impacting her overall well-being and that she needed to make a change. Motivated by the desire to improve her health and reclaim control of her life, Lisa embarked on a determined journey towards quitting smoking once and for all.

Effective Quitting Strategies:

Setting a Clear Goal:
Lisa began her journey by setting a clear and specific goal of quitting smoking within a defined timeframe. By establishing this goal, she created a tangible target to work towards, which helped her stay motivated and focused throughout her quitting process.

Creating a Supportive Network:
Recognizing the importance of a strong support system, Lisa reached out to her family, friends, and even joined a local smoking cessation support group. Sharing her struggles with others who understood her challenges provided the emotional support she needed, and the accountability to stay committed to her goal.

Developing Healthy Coping Mechanisms:
To replace the reliance on cigarettes as a coping mechanism, Lisa explored alternative methods for managing stress and dealing with her emotions. She discovered the benefits of exercise, meditation,

and engaging in creative hobbies, such as painting and writing. These healthy coping mechanisms not only helped her distract herself from cravings but also provided a sense of fulfillment and satisfaction.

Utilizing Nicotine Replacement Therapy:
Recognizing the physical aspect of her addiction, Lisa sought the guidance of a healthcare professional who recommended nicotine replacement therapy (NRT). Through the use of nicotine patches and gum, Lisa gradually weaned herself off nicotine, minimizing withdrawal symptoms and cravings.

Modifying Triggering Environments:
Lisa identified the situations and environments that triggered her cravings and made necessary adjustments. She avoided places where smoking was prevalent and replaced old routines associated with smoking, such as morning coffee with a walk in the park or engaging in deep breathing exercises.

Celebrating Milestones and Rewarding Progress:
Throughout her quitting journey, Lisa celebrated each milestone achieved and rewarded herself with small, meaningful treats. By acknowledging her progress and giving herself positive reinforcement, she stayed motivated and felt a sense of accomplishment with each passing day.

Results and Transformation:

Through perseverance and the application of these effective quitting strategies, Lisa successfully quit smoking after several months of dedication and hard work. Not only did she notice a significant improvement in her physical health, but she also experienced a newfound sense of self-confidence and control over her life. Lisa's success story serves as a reminder that with determination and the right strategies, anyone can overcome their addictions and transform their lives for the better.

Conclusion:

Lisa's success story exemplifies the power of effective quitting strategies in overcoming addiction. By setting clear goals, building a support network, developing healthy coping mechanisms, utilizing nicotine replacement therapy, modifying triggering environments, and celebrating milestones, individuals can take control of their lives and break free from the chains of addiction. Remember, each journey is unique, but with the right strategies and unwavering determination, you too can achieve success in overcoming your own habits or dependencies.

Exploring different cessation methods (cold turkey, gradual reduction, nicotine replacement therapy)

Cessation methods for quitting smoking can vary depending on individual preferences and needs. Here are three common methods:

Cold Turkey: Cold turkey involves quitting smoking abruptly without any external support or gradual reduction in nicotine intake. It requires strong willpower and determination. While this method can be challenging, some people find it effective because it eliminates nicotine dependency completely. However, it can also lead to strong withdrawal symptoms, making it difficult to maintain long-term abstinence.

Gradual Reduction: Gradual reduction involves gradually decreasing the number of cigarettes smoked over time until eventually quitting completely. This method allows the body to adjust to lower nicotine levels and can help manage withdrawal symptoms more easily. Some individuals find this approach less daunting than quitting cold turkey. However, it requires discipline and may prolong the process of quitting, as it can be challenging to stick to the reduction schedule.

Nicotine Replacement Therapy (NRT): NRT involves using products that deliver nicotine without the harmful chemicals found in cigarettes, such as nicotine patches, gum, lozenges, nasal sprays, and inhalers. These products help reduce withdrawal symptoms and cravings by providing a controlled dose of nicotine. NRT can be an effective method, especially for individuals with strong nicotine addiction. It allows them to gradually wean off nicotine while minimizing withdrawal symptoms. NRT is available over-the-counter or with a prescription, and it's important to follow the recommended usage guidelines.

It's worth noting that individual experiences and preferences vary, so what works for one person may not work for another. It's advisable to consult a healthcare professional or a smoking cessation specialist who can provide personalized advice and support based on your specific situation. They can help you determine the most suitable cessation method and may even recommend a combination of approaches to increase your chances of success.

Here are some additional details about each cessation method:

Cold Turkey:

Pros: Quitting abruptly eliminates nicotine from your system quickly, and it may be a more decisive and empowering approach for some individuals.
Cons: Withdrawal symptoms can be intense, including irritability, cravings, difficulty concentrating, mood swings, and insomnia. It requires significant willpower and may be challenging to sustain long-term abstinence without external support.

Gradual Reduction:

Pros: Reducing the number of cigarettes gradually can help the body adjust to lower nicotine levels and minimize withdrawal symptoms. It may be less overwhelming than quitting abruptly.
Cons: It requires discipline and commitment to stick to the reduction schedule. Some people may find it challenging to maintain motivation and may prolong the quitting process. There is also a risk of returning to previous smoking levels.
Nicotine Replacement Therapy (NRT):

Pros: NRT products provide a controlled dose of nicotine, which helps reduce cravings and withdrawal symptoms. They are available in various forms, allowing flexibility to choose what works best for you. NRT can increase your chances of successfully quitting smoking.
Cons: NRT products still deliver nicotine, so there is a risk of dependence. It's important to follow the recommended usage guidelines and eventually wean off the NRT products to achieve complete nicotine independence. Some people may experience mild side effects such as skin irritation, nausea, or dizziness.
In addition to these methods, there are other cessation resources and support systems available. These include counseling, support groups, online programs, smartphone apps, and prescription medications (such as bupropion or varenicline) that can aid in smoking cessation. Combining different methods or seeking

professional guidance can further enhance your chances of successfully quitting smoking.

Remember, quitting smoking is a journey, and what works for one person may not work for another. It's important to find a method that suits your individual needs and preferences. Be patient, stay motivated, and don't hesitate to seek support from healthcare professionals or dedicated smoking cessation programs.

Cognitive-behavioral techniques for overcoming cravings and managing withdrawal symptoms

Cognitive-behavioral techniques can be highly effective in overcoming cravings and managing withdrawal symptoms. Here are some techniques that can be helpful:

Identify triggers: Pay attention to the situations, people, or emotions that tend to trigger cravings or withdrawal symptoms. By identifying these triggers, you can develop strategies to avoid or cope with them effectively.

Cognitive restructuring: Challenge and reframe your thoughts and beliefs about cravings and withdrawal symptoms. Replace negative or self-defeating thoughts with more positive and empowering ones. For example, instead of thinking, "I can't handle these cravings," you could reframe it as, "Cravings are uncomfortable, but I have the power to overcome them."

Thought stopping: When you notice yourself dwelling on cravings or withdrawal symptoms, use a mental cue or a physical action to interrupt those thoughts. You might say "stop" to yourself or snap a rubber band on your wrist to shift your focus away from the craving.

Distraction techniques: Engage in activities that can divert your attention away from cravings or withdrawal symptoms. This could include hobbies, exercise, reading, listening to music, or spending time with supportive friends or family.

Relaxation techniques: Practice relaxation exercises, such as deep breathing, progressive muscle relaxation, or meditation, to reduce stress and manage withdrawal symptoms. Relaxation techniques can help calm your mind and body, making it easier to resist cravings.

Behavioral strategies: Develop alternative behaviors to replace the urge to engage in the addictive behavior. For example, if you have a craving for cigarettes, you could go for a walk, chew gum, or drink water instead. By substituting healthier behaviors, you can gradually weaken the association between the craving and the addictive behavior.

Social support: Surround yourself with a supportive network of friends, family, or support groups who understand your struggle and can provide encouragement and accountability. Sharing your experiences with others who have gone through similar challenges can be immensely helpful in staying motivated and focused on your recovery.

Self-monitoring: Keep a journal or use a mobile app to track your cravings, withdrawal symptoms, and progress. This self-monitoring can help you identify patterns, understand your triggers better, and celebrate your successes along the way.

Remember, overcoming cravings and managing withdrawal symptoms can be a gradual process. It's essential to be patient and kind to yourself throughout the journey. Consider seeking professional help from a therapist or counselor experienced in addiction if you need additional support.

Here are some additional cognitive-behavioral techniques for overcoming cravings and managing withdrawal symptoms:

Imagery techniques: Use guided imagery or visualization exercises to create mental images that promote relaxation, self-control, and resilience. For example, imagine yourself successfully resisting a craving or visualize a healthier and happier future without the addictive behavior.

Problem-solving skills: Develop effective problem-solving skills to address the underlying issues that may contribute to cravings and withdrawal symptoms. Identify any obstacles or challenges that may arise during your recovery journey and brainstorm practical solutions to overcome them.

Reframing and reappraisal: Practice reframing your perspective on cravings and withdrawal symptoms by viewing them as signs of healing and progress rather than as unbearable hardships. Reframe them as opportunities for personal growth and self-improvement.

Assertiveness training: Learn assertiveness skills to express your needs and boundaries confidently. Assertiveness can help you resist pressure from others to engage in addictive behaviors and communicate your decision to change effectively.

Self-reward system: Set up a reward system for yourself to celebrate milestones and achievements along your recovery journey. This could involve treating yourself to something you enjoy or engaging in a pleasurable activity as a way to reinforce positive behavior.

Mindfulness techniques: Practice mindfulness meditation and mindfulness-based stress reduction techniques. Being fully present in the moment without judgment can help you observe cravings and withdrawal symptoms without giving in to them.

Mindfulness can also enhance your self-awareness and strengthen your ability to make conscious choices.

Education and psychoeducation: Learn about the physiological and psychological aspects of addiction and withdrawal symptoms. Educate yourself about the potential challenges you may face, the recovery process, and the benefits of overcoming addiction. This knowledge can empower you and provide a sense of control over your recovery.

Relapse prevention planning: Develop a relapse prevention plan that outlines strategies to cope with high-risk situations and prevent relapse. Identify warning signs, create coping mechanisms, and establish a support system to help you stay on track.

Remember, each individual is unique, and what works for one person may not work for another. It's important to explore different techniques and find the ones that resonate with you. Consider seeking professional guidance from a therapist or counselor specializing in addiction if you need personalized support in overcoming cravings and managing withdrawal symptoms.

Utilizing mindfulness practices to reduce stress and increase self-awareness:

Mindfulness practices are indeed effective in reducing stress and increasing self-awareness. By cultivating mindfulness, individuals can develop a greater sense of presence, attention, and acceptance in their daily lives. Here are some mindfulness practices that can help you achieve these goals:

Mindful Breathing: Take a few moments to focus on your breath. Pay attention to the sensation of the breath as it enters and leaves your body. If your mind wanders, gently bring it back to the breath. This practice can help calm the mind and bring you into the present moment.

Body Scan: Close your eyes and bring your attention to different parts of your body, starting from your toes and moving up to your head. Notice any sensations or areas of tension without judgment. This practice promotes relaxation and body awareness.

Mindful Walking: Go for a walk and pay attention to each step you take. Feel the ground beneath your feet, the movement of your body, and the sensations in your muscles. Engage your senses by noticing the sights, sounds, and smells around you.

Mindful Eating: Slow down and savor each bite of your meal. Notice the flavors, textures, and smells. Pay attention to the process of chewing and swallowing. Eating mindfully can enhance your enjoyment of food and help you develop a healthier relationship with eating.

Mindful Observation: Choose an object in your environment, such as a flower, a piece of art, or a natural scene. Study it closely, noticing its details, colors, and shapes. Allow yourself to fully engage with the present moment and let go of any distracting thoughts.

Loving-Kindness Meditation: Sit comfortably and silently repeat phrases of well-wishes for yourself and others. Start with yourself, then extend your wishes to loved ones, acquaintances, and even to those you have difficulties with. This practice cultivates compassion, empathy, and connection.

Consistency is key when practicing mindfulness. Start with short sessions and gradually increase the duration over time. You can integrate mindfulness into your daily routine by choosing specific moments or activities to be more present and aware. With regular practice, you'll likely experience reduced stress, improved focus, and heightened self-awareness.

Here are some additional mindfulness practices that can further support stress reduction and increase self-awareness:

Mindful Journaling: Set aside time each day to write down your thoughts, feelings, and experiences without judgment or censorship. This practice can help you gain insights into your emotions, patterns of thinking, and areas of personal growth.

Mindful Listening: During conversations or when listening to music, give your full attention to the sounds and words being spoken. Avoid the tendency to formulate responses in your mind and instead focus on truly understanding and empathizing with the speaker.

Mindful Media Consumption: Be conscious of how you engage with media, such as social media, news, and entertainment. Notice how certain content makes you feel and whether it aligns with your values. Take breaks from excessive screen time and choose media that nourishes your well-being.

Mindful Pause: Throughout the day, take short breaks to pause, breathe, and check in with yourself. Observe your thoughts, emotions, and physical sensations without judgment. This practice can help you respond consciously rather than react automatically to situations.

Mindful Gratitude: Take a few moments each day to reflect on and express gratitude for the positive aspects of your life. This practice can shift your focus to what is going well and foster a greater sense of contentment and appreciation.

Mindful Self-Compassion: Treat yourself with kindness and understanding, especially during challenging times. Notice your inner dialogue and replace self-criticism with self-compassion. Practice accepting yourself as you are, with all your strengths and imperfections.

Remember that mindfulness is not about eliminating stress or achieving a particular state of mind. It's about developing an open and non-judgmental awareness of your present moment experience. Regular practice and patience are key to experiencing the full benefits of mindfulness in reducing stress and increasing self-awareness.

Chapter 5

Finding Support system

In this chapter, we will explore the crucial role that support plays in helping individuals quit smoking. We will follow the inspiring journey of Sarah, a former smoker who successfully quit with the help of support networks. Her story illustrates the importance of finding the right support system and utilizing available resources to overcome the challenges of quitting smoking.

Sarah's Struggle:

Sarah had been a smoker for more than a decade. She started smoking in her late teens, initially as a way to fit in with her peers. Over the years, her habit grew stronger, and smoking became deeply ingrained in her daily routine. Sarah was aware of the harmful effects of smoking on her health, but quitting seemed like an insurmountable task.

The Turning Point:

One day, Sarah experienced a health scare. She developed a persistent cough and found it increasingly difficult to catch her breath. Fear crept into her mind as she realized the potential consequences of her smoking habit. Determined to regain control of her health, she made the life-changing decision to quit smoking.

Seeking Support:

Recognizing that she couldn't do it alone, Sarah began her search for support. She reached out to her family and friends, explaining her desire to quit smoking and asking for their encouragement and understanding. Their positive response filled her with hope and reassurance.

Sarah also discovered a wealth of resources available online and in her community. She joined online support groups, where she connected with others who were going through similar struggles. The shared experiences and collective wisdom of these groups became an invaluable source of motivation and guidance for her.

Professional Help:

To further enhance her chances of success, Sarah sought professional assistance. She scheduled an appointment with a healthcare provider who specialized in smoking cessation. The healthcare provider created a personalized quit plan tailored to Sarah's needs and recommended appropriate nicotine replacement therapies and medications to help manage withdrawal symptoms.

Supportive Therapies:

In addition to medical intervention, Sarah explored various supportive therapies to address the psychological aspects of her addiction. She attended counseling sessions, both individually and in group settings, which helped her uncover underlying emotional triggers that drove her to smoke. Through therapy, she developed coping strategies and learned healthier ways to manage stress and cravings.

Celebrating Milestones:

As Sarah progressed on her journey to quit smoking, she celebrated every milestone, no matter how small. Each smoke-free day became an accomplishment worth acknowledging. She rewarded herself with non-smoking related treats, such as a relaxing day at the spa, a favorite book, or a night out with friends. These rewards reinforced her determination and provided positive reinforcement.

Staying Accountable:

Sarah understood the importance of accountability in her quest to quit smoking. She confided in her close friends and family, updating them regularly on her progress. Knowing that others were invested in her success kept her motivated and encouraged her to stay strong, even during challenging moments.

Embracing a Healthy Lifestyle:

Quitting smoking inspired Sarah to adopt a healthier lifestyle overall. She began exercising regularly, focusing on activities that helped alleviate stress and distract her from cravings. She also made conscious efforts to eat nutritious meals and drink plenty of water. These lifestyle changes not only improved her physical well-being but also strengthened her resolve to remain smoke-free.

Conclusion:

Sarah's success story demonstrates the power of support in overcoming the addiction to smoking. By leveraging the support of loved ones, seeking professional help, and utilizing various resources, she conquered the challenges and emerged as a smoke-free individual.

If you are on a journey to quit smoking, take inspiration from Sarah's story. Reach out to your support network, access available resources, and embrace the guidance of healthcare professionals. Remember, you are not alone, and with the right support, you can achieve a smoke-free life.

Engaging with friends, family, and support networks on how to quit smoking

Quitting smoking is a commendable decision, and engaging with friends, family, and support networks can significantly increase your chances of success. Here are some ways to involve them in your journey to quit smoking:

Share your decision: Start by informing your close friends, family members, and supportive individuals about your intention to quit smoking. Explain why it's important to you and ask for their understanding and encouragement.

Seek emotional support: Let your loved ones know that you may experience challenges and cravings during the quitting process. Ask them to provide emotional support and understanding when you need it the most.

Ask for accountability: Request your friends and family to hold you accountable for your decision. This can involve checking in with you regularly, reminding you of your commitment, and celebrating your progress.

Avoid smoking triggers together: Identify common situations or places that trigger your urge to smoke and ask your friends and family to help you avoid them. For example, if socializing at a specific venue often leads to smoking, suggest alternative activities or locations where smoking is less prevalent.

Encourage healthy activities: Engage in activities that promote health and well-being, such as exercise, hiking, or pursuing hobbies, with your friends and family. These activities not only distract you from smoking but also strengthen your relationships with them.

Seek support groups: Joining a support group or attending smoking cessation programs can provide you with additional resources and a network of individuals who are going through similar challenges. These groups can offer guidance, advice, and a sense of community to help you stay motivated.

Celebrate milestones: Share your progress and celebrate milestones with your friends and family. Whether it's one week, one month, or one year smoke-free, their acknowledgment and encouragement can boost your confidence and motivation.

Educate them about quitting methods: Share information about different quitting methods and therapies with your loved ones. This can help them understand the strategies you're employing and enable them to provide more informed support.

Remember that quitting smoking can be a challenging process, and having a strong support network can make a significant difference. Stay committed, seek help when needed, and lean on your friends and family for encouragement and assistance throughout your journey

Here are some additional ways to engage with friends, family, and support networks to help you quit smoking:

Involve them in your quit plan: Share your quit plan with your loved ones and ask for their input. They may have suggestions or ideas that can enhance your strategy. Involving them in the planning process makes them feel invested in your success.

Create a smoke-free environment: Request that your friends and family maintain a smoke-free environment when you're around. This means not smoking in your presence and refraining from offering you cigarettes or smoking paraphernalia.

Seek distraction techniques: Ask your support network to help you find healthy distractions when you experience cravings. They can engage you in conversations, activities, or games to divert your attention away from smoking.

Encourage open communication: Foster open and honest communication with your loved ones. Let them know how you're feeling during the quitting process, including any challenges or triggers you encounter. Their understanding and support can make a significant difference.

Set up rewards or incentives: Work together with your friends and family to establish a reward system for reaching specific milestones or staying smoke-free for a certain period. These rewards can serve as motivation and reinforce positive behavior.

Encourage healthy habits: Ask your support network to engage in healthy habits with you, such as exercising, eating nutritious meals, or practicing stress-relieving activities like yoga or meditation. These lifestyle changes can support your overall well-being and help you stay smoke-free.

Be open to their feedback: Your friends and family may observe changes in your behavior or mood during the quitting process. Remain open to their feedback and suggestions, as they may provide valuable insights and offer support based on their observations.

Share educational resources: Provide your loved ones with educational materials or resources about the harmful effects of smoking and the benefits of quitting. This can help them understand the importance of your decision and encourage them to support you further.

Celebrate together: Celebrate significant milestones in your quitting journey with your support network. This can include organizing a small gathering or having a meaningful conversation to acknowledge and appreciate your progress.

Remember that each person's quitting journey is unique, and the level of involvement from your support network may vary. Communication, empathy, and understanding are key to fostering a supportive environment that encourages your efforts to quit smoking successfully.

Joining smoking cessation programs and online communities:

Joining smoking cessation programs and online communities can be highly beneficial for individuals who want to quit smoking. These programs and communities provide a supportive and understanding environment where you can connect with others who are going through similar challenges and share your experiences. Here are some reasons why joining these programs and communities can be helpful:

Support and Accountability: Quitting smoking can be difficult, and having a support system in place can make a significant difference. By joining a smoking cessation program or online community, you can connect with people who understand the struggles and can offer encouragement, advice, and motivation to stay smoke-free. You can also find accountability partners who will help you stay on track and hold you responsible for your quit journey.

Access to Resources: These programs and communities often provide a wealth of resources to help you quit smoking successfully. You can find information about different quitting methods, strategies to cope with cravings and withdrawal symptoms, tips for managing stress, and more. Many programs also offer online tools, such as quitting trackers, personalized plans, and quit smoking apps, which can enhance your chances of success.

Education and Expert Guidance: Smoking cessation programs often have trained professionals, such as doctors, counselors, or smoking cessation specialists, who can provide expert guidance and support. They can offer evidence-based strategies and interventions tailored to your specific needs. These experts can educate you about the health risks of smoking, the benefits of quitting, and the various approaches to quitting smoking, such as nicotine replacement therapy, medications, or behavioral therapies.

Peer Learning and Experiences: Being part of a community of individuals who are going through a similar journey can provide valuable insights and learnings. You can share your experiences, learn from others' successes and challenges, and gain inspiration from their stories. Seeing others who have successfully quit smoking can instill hope and belief in your ability to quit as well.

Online Convenience: Online communities and programs offer the advantage of convenience, especially for those with busy schedules or limited access to in-person resources. You can participate in discussions, seek support, and access resources from the comfort of your home or wherever you have internet access. Online communities often operate 24/7, allowing you to connect with others at any time that suits you.

When considering joining a smoking cessation program or online community, look for reputable organizations or platforms that offer evidence-based information, have positive user reviews, and provide a supportive and non-judgmental environment. Remember that these programs and communities can be a valuable supplement to your quit smoking journey, but it's essential to consult with healthcare professionals for personalized advice and guidance.

Here are a few more points to consider regarding joining smoking cessation programs and online communities:

Coping Strategies and Peer Support: Smoking cessation programs and communities can provide you with coping strategies to manage cravings, handle triggers, and deal with the challenges of quitting smoking. You can learn from others who have successfully quit or are currently in the process, gaining practical tips and techniques to navigate difficult situations. Peer support can be particularly helpful during challenging times when you may feel tempted to relapse.

Non-Judgmental Environment: These programs and communities offer a non-judgmental space where you can openly discuss your struggles, setbacks, and successes without fear of criticism or stigma. Sharing your journey with others who understand can alleviate feelings of isolation and help you stay motivated and committed to quitting smoking.

Motivation and Inspiration: Engaging with a community of individuals who are committed to quitting smoking can provide a constant source of motivation and inspiration. Seeing others achieve their goals and celebrate milestones can ignite your own determination to succeed. Additionally, you can share your progress and celebrate your achievements with others, reinforcing your commitment to a smoke-free life.

Access to Professional Support: Many smoking cessation programs and online communities have healthcare professionals, counselors, or quit coaches who can provide personalized support and guidance. They can answer your questions, address concerns, and offer evidence-based advice to help you overcome challenges and stay on track.

Long-Term Support: Quitting smoking is not just about the initial phase; it's about maintaining a smoke-free lifestyle in the long run. Smoking cessation programs and online communities can offer ongoing support even after you've quit, ensuring that you have the resources and assistance you need to sustain your smoke-free journey.

Tailored Programs and Resources: Different people have different needs when it comes to quitting smoking. Many programs and communities offer customized approaches based on your specific circumstances, preferences, and smoking patterns. This tailored approach can increase the effectiveness of your quit attempts and provide you with strategies that align with your unique situation.

Remember, while joining smoking cessation programs and online communities can be incredibly helpful, quitting smoking is a personal journey, and it's essential to find the strategies and support that work best for you. Combining these resources with professional guidance, such as consulting with healthcare providers or seeking counseling, can enhance your chances of successfully quitting smoking and improving your overall health and well-being.

Seeking professional help and counseling options:
If you're seeking professional help and counseling options, there are several resources available to you. Here are some common options:

Mental health professionals: Reach out to psychologists, psychiatrists, therapists, or counselors who specialize in the specific area you're seeking help for. They can provide individual, couples, or family therapy depending on your needs. You can find professionals through online directories, recommendations from your doctor, or referrals from friends and family.

Online counseling platforms: There are numerous online platforms that offer counseling services via video calls, phone calls, or text messaging. Examples include BetterHelp, Talkspace, and 7 Cups. These platforms provide convenient and accessible options for counseling, especially if you prefer remote sessions.

Employee Assistance Programs (EAP): If you have an employee benefits package, check if it includes an EAP. EAPs often provide short-term counseling services to employees and their families. They can assist with a wide range of personal and work-related issues.

Community mental health centers: Many communities have mental health centers or clinics that offer low-cost or sliding-scale fee services. These centers may have psychologists, therapists, or counselors who provide counseling for individuals who may not have access to private mental health services.

University or college counseling centers: If you're a student, your educational institution may have counseling services available to you. These services are often free or provided at a reduced cost for students. Reach out to your campus counseling center for more information.

Support groups: Support groups can be helpful for certain issues or conditions. They provide a space to connect with others who may be going through similar experiences. Local community centers, nonprofit organizations, or online communities often host support groups.

Remember, it's essential to find a counselor or therapist who you feel comfortable with and who specializes in the specific area you need help with. Don't hesitate to reach out to multiple professionals to find the right fit for you.

Chapter 6

The Role of Medications and Therapies in Quitting Smoking

In the journey to quit smoking, individuals often face various challenges. While sheer determination and willpower play a crucial role in overcoming this addiction, the use of medications and therapies can significantly enhance the chances of success. In this chapter, we will explore the important role that medications and therapies play in helping individuals quit smoking. Through the success story of Mark, we will witness how these interventions can make a positive difference in one's journey towards a smoke-free life.

Mark's Success Story:
Mark was a devoted smoker for over a decade. He had attempted to quit smoking multiple times, but the addictive grip of nicotine always seemed to pull him back. Frustrated by the vicious cycle, he decided to seek professional help. Mark visited a smoking cessation clinic where he received guidance on various medications and therapies available to assist him in his quitting journey.

Medications for Smoking Cessation:
One of the first steps Mark took was to discuss his options with a healthcare professional. They informed him about two commonly prescribed medications for smoking cessation: nicotine replacement therapy (NRT) and prescription medications such as varenicline and bupropion.

Nicotine Replacement Therapy:
Mark's healthcare provider suggested trying NRT, which includes nicotine patches, gum, lozenges, nasal sprays, and inhalers. Mark opted for the nicotine patch, which provided a steady release of nicotine throughout the day, reducing his cravings and withdrawal symptoms. The gradual decrease in nicotine dosage allowed Mark to wean himself off cigarettes without experiencing severe withdrawal symptoms.

Prescription Medications:
Mark's healthcare provider also discussed the option of prescription medications. Varenicline, a medication that reduces nicotine cravings and blocks the rewarding effects of smoking, was recommended. Another option was bupropion, an antidepressant that helps reduce cravings and withdrawal symptoms. Mark and his healthcare provider decided that varenicline would be the most suitable option for him.

Mark's Experience with Medications:

With the aid of the nicotine patch and varenicline, Mark experienced a significant reduction in his cravings and withdrawal symptoms. The patch provided him with a consistent level of nicotine, curbing his urge to smoke. Varenicline helped reduce the pleasure he associated with smoking, making it easier for him to resist the temptation.

Behavioral Therapies:
Apart from medications, Mark's smoking cessation clinic also offered various behavioral therapies to address the psychological aspects of his addiction. Two prominent therapies discussed were cognitive-behavioral therapy (CBT) and motivational interviewing (MI).

Cognitive-Behavioral Therapy:
CBT is a widely used therapy for smoking cessation. Mark participated in CBT sessions that focused on identifying triggers, developing coping strategies, and changing negative thought patterns related to smoking. Through CBT, Mark learned to replace his smoking habit with healthier alternatives and developed skills to manage cravings and stress without relying on cigarettes.

Motivational Interviewing:
Motivational interviewing is a patient-centered approach that helps individuals explore their motivations, strengths, and barriers to quitting smoking. Mark engaged in motivational interviewing

sessions, where he collaborated with a therapist to set personalized goals, enhance his motivation, and strengthen his commitment to quitting. This therapy helped him build confidence and belief in his ability to overcome the addiction.

Combining Medications and Therapies:
Mark's success story demonstrates the power of combining medications and therapies in smoking cessation. The medications helped him overcome physical cravings, while the therapies addressed the psychological and behavioral aspects of his addiction. This comprehensive approach increased Mark's chances of success and provided him with the tools needed to sustain a smoke-free lifestyle.

Conclusion:
The journey to quit smoking can be challenging, but the use of medications and therapies can significantly improve one's chances of success. Mark's success story serves as a testament to the effectiveness of these interventions. By incorporating medications like NRT and varenicline, along with therapies such as CBT and motivational interviewing, individuals can overcome both the physical and psychological aspects of smoking addiction. With the right support and determination, anyone can embark on their own success story and enjoy the numerous health benefits of a smoke-free life

Exploring pharmacological aids for smoking cessation (nicotine replacement therapy, prescription medications)

Pharmacological aids, including nicotine replacement therapy (NRT) and prescription medications, play a crucial role in smoking cessation by helping individuals manage nicotine withdrawal symptoms and reduce cravings. Here's an overview of these treatment options:

Nicotine Replacement Therapy (NRT): NRT involves using products that deliver nicotine to the body without the harmful effects of tobacco smoke. Common NRT products include nicotine patches, gum, lozenges, inhalers, and nasal sprays. These products provide a controlled dose of nicotine, gradually reducing dependence and allowing individuals to focus on breaking the habit of smoking. NRT can help manage withdrawal symptoms, such as cravings, irritability, and difficulty concentrating.

Prescription Medications: There are two main types of prescription medications approved for smoking cessation:

a. Bupropion (Zyban): Originally developed as an antidepressant, bupropion was found to help people quit smoking. It works by reducing cravings and withdrawal symptoms. Bupropion should be started one to two weeks before the quit date and continued for several months.

b. Varenicline (Chantix): Varenicline is a medication that targets the nicotine receptors in the brain, reducing the rewarding effects of smoking and decreasing cravings. It also helps to alleviate withdrawal symptoms. Varenicline is usually started one week before the quit date and taken for a prescribed duration.

Both bupropion and varenicline have been shown to improve smoking cessation rates when used as part of a comprehensive quit-smoking program that includes behavioral support.

It's important to note that medications and therapies are most effective when used in conjunction with behavioral interventions, such as counseling or support groups. These interventions can address the psychological and behavioral aspects of smoking addiction, provide motivation, and help individuals develop coping strategies for triggers and cravings.

Before starting any medication or therapy, it's crucial to consult with a healthcare professional who can evaluate your specific situation, provide personalized recommendations, and monitor your progress to ensure the most effective and safe treatment approach.

Here's some additional information on the role of medications and therapies in smoking cessation:

Combination Therapy: Combining different pharmacological aids can enhance the chances of successfully quitting smoking. For instance, combining nicotine replacement therapy (such as patches or gum) with prescription medications like bupropion or varenicline has shown better results compared to using either approach alone. Combination therapy addresses both the physical and psychological aspects of nicotine addiction.

Behavioral Therapies: Alongside medication, behavioral therapies are essential components of comprehensive smoking cessation programs. These therapies help individuals understand and modify the behaviors, thoughts, and emotions associated with smoking. They can include:

a. Cognitive-Behavioral Therapy (CBT): CBT helps individuals identify and change the negative thought patterns and behaviors that contribute to smoking. It provides coping strategies, problem-solving techniques, and relapse prevention skills.

b. Motivational Interviewing: This technique involves collaborative conversations that enhance motivation and commitment to quitting smoking. Motivational interviewing aims to resolve ambivalence and increase readiness for change.

c. Support Groups: Participating in support groups or counseling sessions can provide a supportive and understanding environment where individuals can share their experiences, receive encouragement, and learn from others who are going through a similar journey.

Mobile Apps and Online Programs: With advancements in technology, various mobile apps and online programs are available to assist individuals in quitting smoking. These resources may include quit plans, tracking tools, reminders, educational materials, and even social support networks. They can be accessed conveniently and provide additional support alongside other interventions.

Remember that the effectiveness of different medications and therapies can vary from person to person. It's essential to work with healthcare professionals who can assess your individual needs and tailor a treatment plan accordingly. They can help determine the most suitable medications, therapy options, and dosage/duration of treatment based on factors such as your smoking history, overall health, and any existing medical conditions. Quitting smoking is a challenging journey, but with the right support, strategies, and persistence, it is possible to achieve success.

Evaluating the effectiveness of alternative therapies (acupuncture, hypnosis, etc.)

Evaluating the effectiveness of alternative therapies for quitting smoking, such as acupuncture and hypnosis, requires considering scientific research and available evidence. While these therapies have been explored as potential methods for smoking cessation, it's important to note that the overall evidence base and the effectiveness of these approaches are still subject to ongoing research and debate.

Acupuncture: Acupuncture involves the insertion of thin needles into specific points on the body. Some studies have suggested that acupuncture may help reduce nicotine cravings and withdrawal symptoms. However, the evidence is mixed, with some studies showing positive effects while others show no significant difference compared to a control group. More high-quality, well-designed studies are needed to draw definitive conclusions.

Hypnosis: Hypnotherapy aims to modify a person's thoughts, feelings, and behaviors through a relaxed state of consciousness. The effectiveness of hypnosis for smoking cessation is also inconclusive. Some studies have shown positive results, indicating that hypnosis can aid in reducing smoking, while others have not found significant benefits. The placebo effect and individual variations in responsiveness to hypnosis may play a role in the mixed findings. Further research is necessary to determine its true effectiveness.

It's important to note that quitting smoking is a complex process, and different approaches work for different individuals. The most effective and widely supported method for quitting smoking is a combination of behavioral counseling and FDA-approved medications like nicotine replacement therapy or prescription medications (e.g., bupropion or varenicline). These methods have undergone extensive scientific evaluation and have shown consistent efficacy in aiding smoking cessation.

If you're considering alternative therapies to quit smoking, it's advisable to consult with a healthcare professional who can provide guidance and help you make an informed decision based on your specific circumstances and medical history. They can also provide recommendations regarding evidence-based treatments and support services available to assist you

Here are a few more alternative therapies that have been explored for smoking cessation:

Mindfulness-Based Therapies: Mindfulness-based therapies, such as mindfulness-based stress reduction (MBSR) or mindfulness-based relapse prevention (MBRP), involve training individuals to develop present-moment awareness and nonjudgmental acceptance of their thoughts and experiences. Some studies have shown that mindfulness-based interventions can be helpful in reducing smoking cravings and promoting abstinence. However, more research is needed to establish their effectiveness compared to standard treatments.

Herbal Remedies: Certain herbal remedies, such as lobelia, St. John's wort, or passionflower, have been suggested as aids for smoking cessation. However, the evidence for their effectiveness is limited, and they should not be considered as stand-alone treatments. It's important to note that herbal remedies can have side effects and may interact with other medications, so consulting with a healthcare professional is advised.

Nicotine-Free Electronic Cigarettes: Nicotine-free electronic cigarettes, also known as e-cigarettes or vapes, have been proposed as a harm reduction tool for quitting smoking. While they eliminate nicotine dependence, the long-term safety and effectiveness of using e-cigarettes for smoking cessation are still under investigation. Additionally, it's worth noting that using e-cigarettes may introduce new risks and can potentially lead to a dual dependence on both e-cigarettes and traditional cigarettes.

Cognitive-Behavioral Therapy (CBT): While not considered an alternative therapy, CBT is a widely studied and evidence-based approach for smoking cessation. CBT helps individuals identify and change the thoughts and behaviors associated with smoking. It can be used alone or in combination with other treatments, such as medication, to increase the chances of successful quitting.

Remember that quitting smoking is a challenging process, and no single therapy or approach guarantees success. It's often beneficial to combine different strategies and seek professional support to enhance your chances of quitting and maintaining abstinence. Consulting with healthcare professionals or seeking assistance from smoking cessation programs can provide personalized guidance and increase your chances of success.

Consulting healthcare professionals for personalized treatment options on how to quit smoking

Quitting smoking can be challenging, but with the right support and resources, it is possible. It's always recommended to consult with healthcare professionals for personalized advice and treatment options that suit your specific needs. Here are some steps you can take:

Talk to your doctor: Schedule an appointment with your primary care physician or a healthcare professional who specializes in smoking cessation. They can assess your health, discuss your smoking history, and provide personalized advice and recommendations.

Explore different cessation methods: There are various methods available to help you quit smoking, including nicotine replacement therapy (NRT), prescription medications, and behavioral therapies. Your healthcare professional can discuss these options with you and help determine which approach is best for you based on your medical history and preferences.

Consider counseling or support groups: Behavioral therapies, such as individual counseling or support groups, can be effective in helping you quit smoking. These programs provide guidance, encouragement, and strategies to overcome challenges during the quitting process.

Develop a quit plan: Work with your healthcare professional to develop a personalized quit plan. This plan may include setting a quit date, identifying triggers and coping strategies, and establishing a support network.

Get support from loved ones: Inform your friends, family, and coworkers about your decision to quit smoking. Their support and understanding can make a significant difference in your journey.

Make lifestyle changes: Alongside quitting smoking, adopting a healthier lifestyle can improve your chances of success. Engage in regular physical activity, eat a balanced diet, manage stress, and get enough sleep.

Stay motivated and persistent: Quitting smoking is a process that may involve setbacks. It's important to stay motivated and persistent, even if you experience relapses. Seek support from healthcare professionals, friends, or support groups to help you stay on track.

Remember, quitting smoking is a highly personal journey, and what works for one person may not work for another. Working closely with healthcare professionals will ensure that you receive personalized advice and treatment options tailored to your needs.

Here are some additional tips and resources to support your journey to quit smoking:

Consider nicotine replacement therapy (NRT): NRT can help reduce withdrawal symptoms by providing controlled amounts of nicotine to your body without the harmful chemicals found in cigarettes. Options include nicotine patches, gum, lozenges, inhalers, and nasal sprays. Your healthcare professional can guide you on the appropriate type and dosage.

Explore prescription medications: There are prescription medications available that can help you quit smoking by reducing cravings and withdrawal symptoms. Common options include bupropion (Zyban) and varenicline (Chantix). Consult with your doctor to see if these medications are suitable for you and to discuss potential side effects.

Utilize smartphone apps and online resources: Numerous smartphone apps and online platforms are designed to support smoking cessation. They can provide motivational messages, track your progress, offer coping strategies, and connect you with a community of individuals going through a similar journey. Some popular apps include QuitNow!, Smoke Free, and Quit Genius.

Join a quit smoking program: Many healthcare facilities and organizations offer structured smoking cessation programs. These programs typically involve a combination of counseling, education, and support. Look for local resources or inquire with your healthcare professional about available programs in your area.

Seek behavioral therapy: Cognitive-behavioral therapy (CBT) is a common approach that helps individuals identify and modify the thoughts and behaviors associated with smoking. CBT can assist in developing strategies to cope with cravings, manage stress, and avoid triggers. Consider seeking out a therapist or counselor who specializes in smoking cessation or addiction.

Stay active and engaged: Engaging in activities that distract you from smoking urges can be helpful. Find hobbies, exercise regularly, or participate in activities that keep your mind occupied and reduce stress. Physical activity has been shown to alleviate withdrawal symptoms and improve mood.

Celebrate milestones and reward yourself: Recognize and reward yourself for your progress. Set milestones, such as being smoke-free for a week or a month, and celebrate your achievements. Treat yourself to something you enjoy or use the money you've saved from not buying cigarettes for something special.

Remember, quitting smoking is a process that requires commitment, support, and patience. Reach out to healthcare professionals who can provide personalized advice and assistance throughout your journey. They can help you develop a comprehensive plan and address any challenges that arise along the way.

Chapter7

Embracing a Smoke-Free Lifestyle

Embracing a smoke-free lifestyle is a commendable decision that can have numerous benefits for your health and overall well-being. Quitting smoking or avoiding tobacco products altogether can significantly improve your quality of life and reduce the risk of various health problems. Here are some steps and tips to help you embrace a smoke-free lifestyle:

Set a quit date: Choose a specific date to stop smoking and mark it on your calendar. Having a target date can help you mentally prepare and commit to your decision.

Seek support: Inform your family, friends, and colleagues about your decision to quit smoking. Their support and encouragement can be invaluable during the challenging moments. You can also join support groups, both online and offline, where you can connect with others who are on the same journey.

Identify triggers: Pay attention to the situations, people, or emotions that trigger your urge to smoke. By identifying these triggers, you can develop strategies to cope with them effectively. For example, if stress triggers your craving for a cigarette, find alternative stress-relief techniques like deep breathing exercises, meditation, or physical activity.

Develop coping mechanisms: Find healthy alternatives to smoking to manage stress or handle cravings. Engage in activities you enjoy, such as exercise, hobbies, or spending time with loved ones. This can help distract your mind and reduce the desire to smoke.

Consider nicotine replacement therapy: Nicotine replacement therapy (NRT) can be helpful in managing withdrawal symptoms. It provides a controlled amount of nicotine to your body, gradually reducing your dependence on it. NRT products include nicotine patches, gum, lozenges, inhalers, and nasal sprays. Consult with a healthcare professional to determine the best option for you.

Stay active: Regular physical activity not only distracts you from smoking but also improves your mood and reduces stress. Aim for at least 30 minutes of moderate-intensity exercise most days of the week. Choose activities you enjoy, such as walking, jogging, swimming, or cycling.

Practice self-care: Taking care of yourself is crucial during the quitting process. Get enough sleep, eat a balanced diet, and engage in activities that promote relaxation and well-being. Consider incorporating stress-management techniques like yoga, deep breathing exercises, or mindfulness meditation into your routine.

Stay positive and resilient: Quitting smoking can be challenging, and it's normal to experience setbacks along the way. If you slip up and have a cigarette, don't be too hard on yourself. Use it as a learning experience and recommit to your smoke-free lifestyle. Celebrate your successes, no matter how small, and focus on the positive changes you're making for your health.

Remember, embracing a smoke-free lifestyle is a journey that requires determination, patience, and support. The benefits of quitting smoking are numerous and long-lasting, ranging from improved lung health, reduced risk of cancer and heart disease, better overall fitness, and increased life expectancy.

Here are some additional tips to help you embrace a smoke-free lifestyle:

Remove smoking triggers: Get rid of cigarettes, lighters, ashtrays, and any other smoking-related items from your surroundings. This can help reduce the temptation to smoke and create a smoke-free environment.

Practice stress management techniques: Find healthy ways to manage stress, as stress can often be a trigger for smoking. Explore relaxation techniques such as deep breathing exercises, progressive muscle relaxation, or engaging in activities that bring you joy and calmness.

Educate yourself: Learn about the negative effects of smoking on your health. Understanding the risks and consequences can strengthen your resolve to stay smoke-free. Research the benefits of quitting smoking and remind yourself of these reasons whenever you feel tempted.

Seek professional help if needed: If you're finding it challenging to quit smoking on your own, don't hesitate to seek professional help. Talk to your healthcare provider about available resources, such as smoking cessation programs, counseling, or medications that can assist you in your journey.

Find healthy alternatives: Instead of reaching for a cigarette, find healthier alternatives to cope with cravings. Chew sugar-free gum, snack on fruits or vegetables, or sip herbal tea. Keeping your hands and mouth occupied can help distract you from the urge to smoke.

Reward yourself: Set milestones and reward yourself when you achieve them. Treat yourself to something you enjoy—a movie night, a new book, or a spa day—as a way to celebrate your progress and reinforce your commitment to a smoke-free lifestyle.

Build a support network: Surround yourself with supportive individuals who can encourage you on your journey. Joining support groups or online communities can provide a sense of camaraderie and understanding, as you connect with others who are going through similar experiences.

Visualize your success: Imagine yourself as a non-smoker, enjoying a healthier and smoke-free life. Visualize the positive changes happening within your body and the benefits you're gaining from your decision to quit smoking. This can help reinforce your motivation and determination.

Be aware of withdrawal symptoms: Understand that withdrawal symptoms, such as irritability, mood swings, and cravings, are temporary and part of the quitting process. Remind yourself that these discomforts will subside over time as your body adjusts to being smoke-free.

Track your progress: Keep a journal or use a quit-smoking app to monitor your progress. Documenting your journey can help you stay accountable, identify patterns or triggers, and reflect on how far you've come.

Remember, embracing a smoke-free lifestyle is a personal choice, and it may take time to fully adjust. Be patient with yourself, stay committed, and focus on the positive changes you're making for your health and well-being.

Rediscovering life without cigarettes

Rediscovering life without cigarettes can be a transformative and empowering journey. Quitting smoking is a significant accomplishment that can improve your health, well-being, and overall quality of life. Here are some tips and insights to help you on this journey:

Motivation: Start by identifying your personal reasons for quitting smoking. It could be for health reasons, financial savings, setting a positive example for loved ones, or regaining control over your life. Keep reminding yourself of these motivations throughout your journey.

Set a quit date: Choose a specific date to quit smoking. This will give you time to prepare mentally and physically. It's essential to pick a day that allows you to minimize potential stressors or triggers.

Seek support: Reach out to your friends, family, and support groups to let them know about your decision to quit smoking. Their encouragement and understanding can be invaluable. Consider joining smoking cessation programs or seeking professional help to enhance your chances of success.

Prepare for withdrawal symptoms: Understand that nicotine withdrawal symptoms are normal and temporary. These symptoms may include irritability, restlessness, difficulty concentrating, cravings, and changes in appetite. Be prepared to manage them by staying hydrated, engaging in physical activity, and using nicotine replacement therapy if recommended by a healthcare professional.

Avoid triggers: Identify situations, people, or places that may trigger the urge to smoke and try to avoid them, especially during the initial days. Modify your routine to reduce exposure to triggers and find healthy alternatives to cope with cravings, such as chewing gum, snacking on healthy foods, or engaging in physical activities.

Find healthy coping mechanisms: Discover new activities and hobbies that can help distract you from the urge to smoke. Exercise regularly, practice deep breathing or meditation, indulge in a creative outlet, or spend quality time with non-smoking friends.

Celebrate milestones: Acknowledge and celebrate your achievements along the way. Reward yourself for staying smoke-free by treating yourself to something enjoyable or investing the money saved on cigarettes into something meaningful.

Stay positive: Quitting smoking is a journey, and setbacks can happen. If you slip and have a cigarette, don't be too hard on yourself. Learn from the experience, recommit to your goal, and continue moving forward. Focus on the progress you've made and the benefits you've already experienced.

Maintain a healthy lifestyle: Adopt a healthy lifestyle to reinforce your commitment to quitting smoking. Eat a balanced diet, exercise regularly, get enough sleep, and manage stress effectively. These habits can boost your overall well-being and help you resist the temptation to smoke.

Stay vigilant: Even after successfully quitting smoking, it's important to stay vigilant. Avoid situations that may trigger relapse, and remind yourself regularly of the reasons why you quit in the first place.

Remember, quitting smoking is a significant achievement, and the benefits of a smoke-free life are immense. Stay committed, be patient with yourself, and embrace the journey of rediscovering life without cigarettes.

Adopting healthy habits and routines to support a smoke-free life:

Adopting healthy habits and routines is crucial to support a smoke-free life. Quitting smoking is a significant step towards improving your overall health and well-being. Here are some healthy habits and routines you can adopt to support your smoke-free journey:

Set a Quit Date: Choose a specific date to quit smoking and stick to it. Having a target date can help you mentally prepare and increase your chances of success.

Seek Support: Inform your family, friends, and loved ones about your decision to quit smoking. Their support and encouragement can make a significant difference. You can also join support groups, both online and offline, to connect with others who are going through the same journey.

Identify Triggers: Understand the situations, emotions, or activities that trigger your urge to smoke. Common triggers include stress, socializing, or certain places. Once you identify them, develop strategies to cope with these triggers without resorting to smoking.

Build a Supportive Environment: Make your home and surroundings smoke-free zones. Get rid of cigarettes, lighters, and ashtrays to minimize temptations. If there are smokers in your household, ask them to support your decision by not smoking around you or keeping their smoking materials out of sight.

Practice Stress Management: Find healthy alternatives to manage stress and relax. Engage in activities such as exercise, meditation, deep breathing exercises, yoga, or hobbies that help you unwind and reduce stress levels.

Exercise Regularly: Physical activity is not only beneficial for your overall health but can also help reduce nicotine cravings and withdrawal symptoms. Engage in regular exercise, such as walking, jogging, swimming, or cycling, for at least 30 minutes a day.

Eat a Balanced Diet: Focus on consuming a nutritious diet that includes fruits, vegetables, whole grains, lean proteins, and healthy fats. Avoid excessive caffeine and alcohol consumption, as they can be associated with increased cravings for cigarettes.

Stay Hydrated: Drink plenty of water throughout the day. Hydration helps flush out toxins from your body and can also help reduce cravings.

Find Healthy Distractions: When cravings strike, distract yourself with activities you enjoy. Read a book, listen to music, solve puzzles, or engage in a hobby that keeps your mind occupied.

Celebrate Milestones: Acknowledge and reward yourself for achieving milestones along your smoke-free journey. Treat yourself to something you enjoy, like a movie night, a spa day, or a small gift. Celebrating your progress can help motivate you to stay on track.

Remember, quitting smoking is a process, and there may be challenges along the way. If you experience setbacks, don't be too hard on yourself. Stay positive, learn from any relapses, and continue to strive for a smoke-free life.

Exploring new hobbies, exercise routines, and stress management techniques

Exploring new hobbies, exercise routines, and stress management techniques can bring a lot of joy and balance to your life. Here are some ideas to get you started:

Hobbies:

Photography: Grab a camera or use your smartphone to capture beautiful moments and explore the world through a lens.
Painting or drawing: Tap into your creativity and express yourself through art. You can try different mediums like watercolors, acrylics, or even digital art.
Cooking or baking: Experiment with new recipes, try different cuisines, and enjoy the process of preparing delicious meals.
Gardening: Cultivate your own garden, whether it's indoors with houseplants or outdoors with flowers, herbs, or vegetables.

Writing: Explore the world of creative writing, journaling, or even start a blog to share your thoughts and experiences.

Exercise Routines:

Yoga: Practice gentle stretches, mindfulness, and relaxation techniques with yoga. It promotes flexibility, strength, and mental well-being.

HIIT workouts: High-Intensity Interval Training (HIIT) involves short bursts of intense exercise followed by periods of rest. It's efficient and helps improve cardiovascular health and burn calories.

Dancing: Join a dance class or follow online tutorials to get moving, improve coordination, and have fun.

Outdoor activities: Explore hiking, cycling, swimming, or any outdoor activity that gets you active and lets you enjoy nature.

Stress Management Techniques:

Meditation: Set aside time each day to meditate, focusing on your breath or using guided meditation apps or videos.

Deep breathing exercises: Practice deep breathing techniques to help calm your mind and reduce stress levels.

Mindfulness: Engage in activities with full presence and awareness, such as mindful eating, walking, or even doing household chores.

Journaling: Write down your thoughts, emotions, and gratitude in a journal to gain clarity and release stress.

Connecting with loved ones: Spend quality time with family and friends, whether it's in person or through phone calls and video chats.

Here are a few more suggestions for hobbies, exercise routines, and stress management techniques:

Hobbies:

Playing a musical instrument: Learn to play the piano, guitar, drums, or any instrument that interests you. It can be a great way to express yourself and relax.
Reading: Dive into the world of literature and explore different genres, authors, and topics. Reading can be both entertaining and enlightening.
Learning a new language: Challenge yourself to learn a new language. You can use language learning apps, online courses, or even join local language exchange groups.
DIY crafts: Engage in DIY (Do-It-Yourself) projects like knitting, crocheting, woodworking, or jewelry making. It's a creative and fulfilling way to spend your time.
Volunteering: Find a cause that you care about and dedicate your time and skills to making a positive impact in your community.
Exercise Routines:

Pilates: Practice Pilates to improve flexibility, core strength, and overall body awareness. There are plenty of online classes and tutorials available for different skill levels.

Martial arts: Join a martial arts class such as karate, taekwondo, or judo. It not only improves physical fitness but also cultivates discipline and self-confidence.

Swimming: Take up swimming as a low-impact exercise that works your entire body. It's refreshing, enjoyable, and beneficial for cardiovascular health.

Team sports: Join a local sports team or club for activities like soccer, basketball, volleyball, or tennis. It's a great way to socialize, compete, and stay fit.

Outdoor adventures: Try rock climbing, kayaking, or paddleboarding to challenge yourself physically while enjoying the beauty of nature.

Stress Management Techniques:

Mindful walking: Take a leisurely walk in nature, paying attention to your surroundings, and focusing on the sensations in your body. It can be calming and rejuvenating.

Aromatherapy: Use essential oils or scented candles to create a soothing atmosphere at home. Scents like lavender, chamomile, or citrus can help promote relaxation.

Progressive muscle relaxation: Practice tensing and relaxing different muscle groups in your body to release tension and promote relaxation. Start from your toes and work your way up to your head.

Time management: Develop effective time management skills to prioritize tasks, set realistic goals, and create a balanced schedule. This can help reduce stress and increase productivity.

Mind-body practices: Explore practices like tai chi, qigong, or Reiki, which focus on harmonizing the mind and body, promoting balance, and reducing stress.

Remember, everyone is different, so feel free to experiment and discover what works best for you. Engaging in hobbies, exercise routines, and stress management techniques is all about finding what brings you joy, relaxation, and a sense of fulfillment. Enjoy the process and embrace the benefits they can bring to your life!